CW01083452

GRACE
WALK
MOMENTS

Steve McVey

HARVEST HOUSE PUBLISHERS
EUGENE, OREGON

Cover by Left Coast Design, Portland, Oregon

Cover painting © CYC / Shutterstock

GRACE WALK MOMENTS
Copyright © 2013 by Steve McVey
Published by Harvest House Publishers
Eugene, Oregon 97402
www.harvesthousepublishers.com

ISBN 978-0-7369-5247-7 (HC)
ISBN 978-0-7369-5248-4 (eBook)

Printed in China

13 14 15 16 17 18 19 20 21 / RDS-JH / 10 9 8 7 6 5 4 3 2 1

This book isn't your regular feel-good devotional. While the things you read here are certain to encourage and warm your heart, I believe they have the potential to do much more than that. The truths in these short devotional chapters can transform you by changing the way you see your heavenly Father, yourself, others, and the world around you. My prayer is that the chapters will both touch and teach you. I believe they can—because that is exactly what happened to me when the Great Teacher began to open the meaning of grace to me in the ways you will read about in *Grace Walk Moments*.

These devotions aren't intended to motivate you to try harder. Instead, they will motivate you to *trust Him*. As you read these chapters you will learn how to stop struggling to advance spiritually and simply rest in His ability to carry you into a stronger, deeper walk of faith. It's amazing. Amazing grace.

The order in which you read the chapters isn't important. I would encourage you to read only one a day and to let what you've read that day incubate in your heart, allowing it to produce fruit in your daily walk. Grace does more than inform you about your faith. It transforms you by His faith operating in your life. It's not about you trying to do better through religious self-improvement. It never has been. It's about Jesus Christ and what *He* can and will do in you, then through you.

Just relax and read in the knowledge that the One who led you to this book will show you what He wants you to glean from it. Don't be surprised to hear your Father's voice in these pages. After all, grace is the language He speaks.

Mighty Things

Call to Me and I will answer you, and I will tell you
great and mighty things, which you do not know.

Jeremiah 33:3

One of the greatest barriers preventing many people from enjoying a life in grace is what they *think* they know. They are firmly entrenched in a paradigm of spiritual reality that to them is self-evident, however imaginary it may actually be. Without divine intervention, the religionist will never experience grace to its fullest extent. Why? Because a religionist is a person who depends on his or her own practices and efforts to gain acceptance with God. Recipients of grace must have a heart and mind that is open toward God—and nothing so decidedly shuts down one's capacity to receive as empty religion.

Many think they understand the truth about grace, yet they have never even begun to comprehend the reality of its beauty in full bloom. Would you be willing to consider for a moment that some of the ideas about the Christian life that you have held as truth may not be grounded in reality? As you continue to grow in your understanding of God's grace, you will see that it is so much bigger and better than you could even imagine. Open yourself to learn, and the Great Teacher who lives in you will show you greater things about Himself than you have ever known.

Recognizing the Source

By His doing you are in Christ Jesus, who became
to us wisdom from God, and righteousness
and sanctification, and redemption.

1 CORINTHIANS 1:30

You will be completely free to rest in your grace walk when you fully understand that it isn't up to you to become a better person by trying hard to do the right things. It is by your Father's doing that you are in Christ Jesus. Jesus has become your wisdom, righteousness, sanctification, and redemption. Your only role is to believe in that reality and rest in Him, refusing to struggle to improve yourself.

This doesn't mean your life is passive. Rather, your lifestyle is one in which you accept the fact that Jesus has done for you all the things you couldn't do in a lifetime of religious commitment and effort. Learn to focus on what He has done and thank Him for His finished work. To the extent that you rest in the reality of what He has already done in you, your experience will increasingly conform to that reality, and you will see your lifestyle be transformed. However, the change won't come by self-effort. It will be by the operation of His grace within you.

Good Works

*We are His workmanship, created in Christ
Jesus for good works, which God prepared
beforehand so that we would walk in them.*

EPHESIANS 2:10

Good works aren't something you have to produce
for God. He has already planned your good works in
advance. Your role is to understand who you are and
live as your authentic self. The word "*workmanship*"
could accurately be translated "*poem*." You are a divine
work of art created by your Father to express the works
He has prepared for you.

You don't have to try to do religious deeds. Simply
be yourself, knowing that good works aren't your gift
to God but are His gift to you. He has already planned
ways for you to honor Him through your actions today.
Go through this day with your spiritual eyes open, and
He will show you the opportunities to glorify Him
through the works He has waiting for you to do. Your
Father will show His love and life to those you encounter—through you, His divine artwork. Relax and allow
Him to show Himself to others through you.

One with Him

The one who joins himself to the
Lord is one spirit with Him.

1 CORINTHIANS 6:17

The idea that Jesus Christ is *in* your life is true—but the news of what grace has accomplished in you is even greater than that. Jesus has so merged Himself into you and you into Him that there is no separation whatsoever. You are a spirit being who has a soul (mind, will, and emotions) and lives in a body. The spirit is the essence of your identity, and it is in that place that Christ has united as one with you.

Think of a cup of coffee. Nobody would say that the cup contains coffee and hot water. The merging of the coffee into the water was so complete when it was brewed that a new identity has emerged in the process. It is now called "coffee." The water's identity has been remade and redefined by the coffee.

So it is with Jesus Christ. He has brought you into union with Him. Your identity has been changed because your very nature has been changed. You aren't just a person with Christ in you. You have been joined to Him as one and the flavor you now have to offer the world is a divine creation.

Affirm Your Holiness

Do you not know that you are a temple of God and that the Spirit of God dwells in you? If any man destroys the temple of God, God will destroy him, for the temple of God is holy, and that is what you are.

1 Corinthians 3:16-17

Trying to become more holy by doing certain things is a common mistake many people make. Consider the temple in the Old Testament. It was considered holy because that's where God lived. Things have changed now. God doesn't live in an Old Testament temple but instead lives inside you. Wherever He lives is made holy by His presence there. That means you are holy, right now at this very moment. Paul didn't suggest that you are to try to become holy but said that you are God's temple and that, since God is holy, that is what you *are.*

You may not feel or even act holy at times, but that's not what determines the truth on this matter. The Spirit of God lives in you, and that alone is what makes you holy. Your need isn't to try to become holy but to recognize that, because of Him, you already are. When you see that, your lifestyle will begin to conform to that truth.

Crucified with Christ

*I have been crucified with Christ; and it is no longer
I who live, but Christ lives in me; and the life which
I now live in the flesh I live by faith in the Son of
God, who loved me and gave Himself up for me.*

GALATIANS 2:20

When Jesus died on the cross, you died with Him. The person you were in Adam was put to death and was buried with Christ. When He arose on the third day, you rose together with Him and now have a new life—His life.

An authentic grace walk is one in which you understand that you don't have to struggle to do the right thing in any situation. Your very existence finds its source in the Son of God, whose total sacrifice shows just how much He loves you. As you rest in Him—in His faith—you will be thrilled to see His life flow out of you.

Paul said, "It is no longer I who live, but Christ lives in me." Take that thought with you through your day today. Watch what a difference it makes to realize that you don't have to handle the challenges you face. Christ, who is inside you, will act through you in every situation.

Freedom from Sin

*Our old self was crucified with Him, in order
that our body of sin might be done away with,
so that we would no longer be slaves to sin.*

ROMANS 6:6

Overcoming sins in your life isn't something that happens by anything you do. It comes as the result of knowing that sin has no actual power over you anymore. The person who loved to sin died with Jesus on the cross. Although temptation is still enticing, the new you loves Him and doesn't want to sin. That's why there's a struggle when you face temptation. If you truly wanted to sin, there would be no struggle. At the heart of who you are, you don't want to sin.

The key to disarming the power of sin in your lifestyle is to embrace the reality that you died to sin. The sin nature that fed itself by sinning no longer exists within you. That's what Paul meant when he referred to the "body of sin" being crucified. Your new nature loves righteousness.

Ask the Holy Spirit to teach you more about this new nature that defines you. As you increasingly see your true identity, the appeal of sin will loosen its grip.

Attaining Righteousness

What shall we say then? That Gentiles, who did not pursue righteousness, attained righteousness, even the righteousness which is by faith; but Israel, pursuing a law of righteousness, did not arrive at that law.

ROMANS 9:30-31

Legalistic religion will tell you that you must pursue righteousness and not give up until you achieve it, but that's not what the Bible says. Paul described how the Gentiles attained righteousness although they did not pursue it. Israel, on the other hand, pursued it vigorously but never reached the goal. These outcomes are the opposite of what you may have been told.

Righteousness isn't something to achieve or earn. It is something you have *received* in Jesus Christ. The reason these Gentiles were made righteous is because they believed in the grace of God. The Jews, however, insisted on trying to gain righteousness through their religious behavior. Which approach have you taken?

Determine at this moment to stop trying to become more righteous through religious activity. Recognize that you are righteous by faith, not by fighting to do the right things. Jesus Christ has made you righteous. Accept it and you will glorify Him by giving Him all the credit for the righteousness you possess.

Religious Rules

While we were in the flesh, the sinful passions,
which were aroused by the Law, were at work in
the members of our body to bear fruit for death.

ROMANS 7:5

The common approach many take to resisting sinful passions is to apply religious rules to themselves. But this verse shows that to take that approach only makes the problem worse. The Bible plainly teaches here that the Law arouses sinful passions. Don't think of the Law as simply meaning Old Testament laws. A legalistic system exists anytime we try to conform to any system of keeping religious rules.

Think of a carbonated drink inside a bottle. If you were to put your thumb over the opening of the bottle and vigorously shake it, what would happen when you took your thumb off? The contents would spew everywhere.

That's what religious rules do in a person's life. A lifestyle that honors God doesn't come by trying to live by rules. Try to squelch sin by observing rules through sheer willpower and it won't be long until sin comes spewing forth out of your life. Instead of focusing on rules, put your attention on the love of your Father for you. Prohibition has never reduced sinning, but Passionate Love will cause you to become so caught up in Him that you don't need rules.

Victory in Jesus

Thanks be to God, who gives us the victory
through our Lord Jesus Christ.

1 CORINTHIANS 15:57

There are no steps, no formulas, and no principles for experiencing victory in your grace walk. There is only one way to experience the life you were intended to live, and that way is found in the person of Jesus Christ. Human independence tries to find a way to make it happen through our own efforts, but we will never know the life we were designed to enjoy if that is the path we follow.

Everything in our culture, including most religious institutions, challenges us to try harder to do better in order to be a better person. Self-made individuals are applauded. The goal of doing our personal best is the mantra of the self-help community.

The Bible, on the other hand, tells us that our Father gives us victory through His Son, Jesus Christ. It's not that you do nothing. You will be active, but first it's a matter of having the right focus. When you focus on Jesus Christ as your source of victory, the actions that follow will be a result of recognizing Him as your life source. You will live *from* victory instead of striving to achieve it by your performance.

God's First Moment
with Mankind

God blessed them; and God said to them,
"Be fruitful and multiply, and fill the earth, and
subdue it; and rule over the fish of the sea
and over the birds of the sky and over every
living thing that moves on the earth."

GENESIS 1:28

The heart of your God is seen in the way He related to mankind immediately after He had created them, during the first moments of Adam and Eve's existence. What was the very first thing He did in His relationship to His highest creation? "God blessed them."

Your concept of your Creator will largely determine the way you relate to Him. If you see Him as a Great Judge who carefully watches your behavior to make sure you're doing the right things, you have misunderstood your Father. God created you to bless you.

The first word He spoke to mankind was, "Be fruitful and multiply." His first word was to speak blessing into their lives. Dead religion presents a false caricature of God, presenting Him as one who is primarily concerned with our behavior. The Bible shows Him as being very different. His concern is simply with you.

Your God wants to bless you today. He speaks words of loving encouragement to you. Go forth into your day with that assurance.

Self-Consciousness

He said, "Who told you that you were naked?"

GENESIS 3:11

When Adam and Eve ate from the forbidden tree in the Garden of Eden, one of the first things that happened was that they became entrapped in a faulty concept of both themselves and their God. Adam and Eve saw their nakedness and hid themselves.

When God came for His daily walk, He called out to Adam and asked, "Where are you?" Adam responded by admitting that he had sinned and was afraid because he was naked. His self-consciousness drove him into hiding. He now felt unacceptable to his Creator.

God's question to Adam is one that may serve you well to answer. "Who told you that you were naked?" or to put it another way, "Who told you that you now aren't acceptable to me?" God had seen Adam naked from the moment He had created him. Adam's sin didn't change God's mind toward him at all, but it changed Adam's mind toward God.

Your sin doesn't change how your Father feels toward you. When you feel unacceptable, run *to* Him and not away from Him. He has seen you at your very worst and still loves you. Refuse to be self-conscious and know that He came to deliver you from sin and into authentic friendship with Him. His love is bigger than your shame.

A Happy Father

The LORD your God is in your midst,
A victorious warrior.
He will exult over you with joy,
He will be quiet in His love,
He will rejoice over you with shouts of joy.

ZEPHANIAH 3:17

Set your mind on the great love that your Father has for you and you'll see it make a huge difference in your daily perspective. God isn't watching your activity from a distance. He is "in your midst" in the daily activity of your life. He stands ready to fight for you because of your great value to Him.

When Zephaniah said that God "will rejoice over you," He was suggesting that God literally dances with joy when He sees you. The Hebrew word for *rejoice* literally means "to twirl with delight." He sings songs of joy when He considers the union you and He share together.

Your feelings may not confirm the reality of this biblical truth, but choose now not to allow your feelings to drive your beliefs. Believe what He has said about you, and stand in faith on that belief every day. As you renew your mind to the truth of how God feels toward you, it will begin to transform your outlook on every detail of your life.

Love's Motivation

We love, because He first loved us.

1 John 4:19

Have you ever prayed for God to help you love Him more? If so, this verse is the answer to your prayer. Every good thing that comes out of your life is the result of His work in you. His response to your desire to love Him more is to cause you to understand better how much He loves you.

None of us can give what we don't know we have. To love others you must know how much you are loved. As you grow in your understanding of the greatness of your Father's love for you, that same love will begin to overflow your life and spill out to Him and to others. There is no love apart from God's love—and as His love fills your consciousness you won't be able to contain it!

The way to love God more or love others more is the same. It's to understand the depth of His love. Open your heart today and receive His love in a fresh and meaningful way. It is the one who knows he or she is deeply loved who loves most.

Growing in Grace

I am confident of this very thing, that
He who began a good work in you will
perfect it until the day of Christ Jesus.

PHILIPPIANS 1:6

The tendency to be critical of ourselves is common to almost everybody. We think that we should be handling life's frustrations better, that our faith should be stronger, that we should be more spiritually mature, and so on. The list goes on and on.

This kind of self-criticism isn't productive in any way. You can no more grow yourself into maturity than a sapling can rush itself into becoming a mighty oak. The work of growth in your life is the work of the Spirit of God who indwells you. He has committed Himself to you—He will not stop what He has begun, but will complete it.

Your role is to simply yield yourself and everything associated with your life into His loving hands. What area of your life frustrates you today? At what point have you thought you should be further along? Let go of your control over those places in life and trust Him to accomplish His purpose in His timing. He will finish what He has started. You can count on it.

Self-Condemnation

*There is now no condemnation for
those who are in Christ Jesus.*

ROMANS 8:1

Self-condemnation is one of the subtlest forms of idolatry. The finished work of Jesus on the cross completely dealt with every sin of your lifetime. He has taken away your sins so thoroughly that it is as if you never committed them. He certainly doesn't condemn you, and the sin that condemned you is gone. There is no condemnation for those who are in Christ Jesus—none.

Self-condemnation comes when we judge ourselves, pass verdict on ourselves, and then impose a sentence on ourselves that requires self-contempt. The whole act suggests that we don't really believe our sins have been completely dealt with by Christ. Self-condemnation comes when we choose to take guilt back upon ourselves and dole out punishment upon ourselves. It is an insult to the reality that the cross has set us free from such a curse.

You may feel that refusing to live in self-condemnation is to take sin lightly. In reality, though, you are expressing faith in the finished work of Jesus Christ in effectively dealing with your sin. Thank God that your sins have been taken away, and glorify Him by refusing to act as if they haven't.

Distracted from Jesus

But Martha was distracted with all her preparations.
LUKE 10:40

The story of Mary and Martha teaches valuable lessons about resting in Christ and about service toward Him. One of the more overlooked aspects of this story is found in the short phrase about Martha being distracted with all her service toward Jesus. From what, or better yet, from whom was she distracted? It was Jesus! Her service actually had drawn her focus away from Him.

Many today find themselves in the same place as Martha. It's easy to become so caught up in what we are trying to do for Jesus that we lose focus on Jesus Himself. Christian service is no substitute for intimacy with Christ.

Have you found yourself busy with service to the point that you're more caught up in what you're doing than you are with the One for whom you seek to do it? When Jesus spoke to Martha about her problem, He told her that *one thing* was necessary and that Mary had discovered it. That one thing is experiencing intimacy with Him.

Spiritual service is to be the overflow of that intimacy. Don't make the mistake of being more preoccupied by what might be called "the work of Christ" than you are with Christ Himself.

Stopping the Thief

The thief comes only to steal and kill and destroy;
I came that they may have life, and have it abundantly.

JOHN 10:10

Contemporary culture makes so many demands on all of us. We often find ourselves mentally, emotionally, and physically exhausted by it all. Do you find yourself caught up in the frenzy of modern life? Do you feel at times like you're on a treadmill that seems to move faster and faster?

That's not the life for which you have been created to live. A frenzied lifestyle steals peace, kills joy, destroys contentment, and robs us of the most meaningful things in life. It promises things that are only temporary at best. Jesus said that it is "the thief" who steals, kills, and destroys. But Jesus came so that you can have life. Not just biological life, but a life that can only be realized in Him.

Are your schedule, commitments, and expenditure of energy robbing you of what is most important? If so, ask your Father to show you how to realign your priorities and how to reallocate your time and energy in a way that prevents you from being robbed of *real* life. He came so that you can experience life to the fullest. And it's a life than can only be realized in Him.

Hearing His Voice

My sheep hear My voice, and I know
them, and they follow Me.

JOHN 10:27

Do you recognize your Father's voice when you hear Him? Jesus said all His sheep hear His voice, but learning to recognize that it *is* the voice of your Shepherd will help you immeasurably in your grace walk. How can you recognize His voice when He speaks?

The most important thing is to want to hear Him. Go through your day with your spiritual ears opened, wanting to hear Him. Realize that He isn't limited to speaking to you through religious means. While Jesus often speaks through the Bible and sermons and spiritual songs, He knows the language of life on this planet too. He can speak to you through the words of friends, through circumstances, through nonreligious songs, through art, through nature, through movies, and in so many other ways that are outside the box of religion.

Ask Him to teach you to identify His voice. Then when He speaks in ways in which you aren't accustomed, don't dismiss it simply because it isn't a religious voice. Nothing He says will stand in contradiction to what He says in Scripture—but remember, not everybody in the world even has a Bible. Your God is speaking to you continuously.

Knowing God

This is eternal life, that they may know You, the only true God, and Jesus Christ whom You have sent.

JOHN 17:3

What is the reason God has given you eternal life? People have different ideas about this, but in this verse Jesus identifies the exact meaning of possessing eternal life. He said we possess eternal life so that we may know His Father and Him.

Your salvation is about one thing: experiencing the knowledge of the Father through the Son in the communion of the Holy Spirit. Our Triune God wants you to rest in the loving embrace of the Trinity so that you will fully know His life and love within you.

There has never been a time when your God didn't have you in His heart and on His mind. He brought you into existence to be loved by Him. When Jesus said that your eternal life is so that you may "know" Him, He uses a powerful word. It's the same word used in Scripture when it says that Mary did not "know" a man until after the birth of Jesus. The word denotes the strongest kind of intimacy.

God knows you fully and loves you dearly. You will spend your lifetime and eternity growing in the knowledge of His great love for you. Rest in that love today and allow it to bring perspective to everything you do.

There Is No West Pole

As far as the east is from the west,
So far has He removed our transgressions from us.

PSALM 103:12

There is an unhealthy obsession with sin in modern Christendom. We preach about sin, discuss sin, think about sin, and study it. Such a focus is neither helpful nor necessary. God has dealt with our sin in such a way that the only response we really need is to believe that our sin is gone and walk in freedom from it.

Our sins have been separated from us as far as the east is from the west. That statement is very revealing. If a person travels north they will eventually find the North Pole and begin to travel south again. If they travel far enough south, they will once again meet north. North and south come together at the poles. However, one can travel east and never find oneself going west again, and vice versa. East and west never meet.

God has separated your sins from you in that way. The chance of your sins being attached to you again is as great as the likelihood of a traveler discovering the West Pole. It won't happen because it can't happen. Your sins are gone and nothing will ever change that.

A Finished Work

Those whom He foreknew, He also predestined to
become conformed to the image of His Son, so that
He would be the firstborn among many brethren;
and these whom He predestined, He also called;
and these whom He called, He also justified; and
these whom He justified, He also glorified.

ROMANS 8:29-30

The working of God to transform your life is all Him. It's not based on anything you do or don't do. This text teaches that your Father knew you before you were ever born. He predestined you to become like His Son, Jesus. That all happened before you were an idea in your parents' minds.

God miraculously called you to Himself and justified you through Jesus Christ. The Bible even says here that He has already glorified you. When God says something is true, it is so certain that we can speak of it in past tense. In "the eternal now" you look like Jesus. You are free from sin and have a righteous standing before God.

How can these things be? It is by His grace. You don't have to struggle to make yourself better. Your God has already done that. The only need now is to grow in your understanding of what He has already accomplished for you and learn how to live each day as your authentic self.

The Greatest Work

*They said to Him, "What shall we do, so that
we may work the works of God?" Jesus answered
and said to them, "This is the work of God, that
you believe in Him whom He has sent."*

JOHN 6:28-29

Perhaps the most emphasized aspect of Christianity today revolves around the works we do for God. Ironically, when the disciples asked Jesus what they could do so that they might be able to do the kind of works He did, the response wasn't a prescription about how to act. Instead, in one short sentence Jesus defined the work of God that matters most—to believe in Jesus.

With all the talk about godly works in the church world of today, the real issue that needs to be emphasized is belief. Do you believe Him when He said He has taken away your sins and will never hold you accountable for them, even when you have committed a terrible sin? Do you believe Him when He says He will never leave or forsake you, even in moments when you can't sense His presence whatsoever? Do you believe that He will work out all the details of your life for your good and for His glory?

To be in the place where Christ can work through you in this world, the greatest thing you can do is to trust Him completely. Yield your life to Him, trust Him, and watch what He will do through you.

Righteous in Christ

As through the one man's disobedience the many
were made sinners, even so through the obedience
of the One the many will be made righteous.

ROMANS 5:19

What Jesus Christ has done for us through His obedience on the cross is certainly enough to overcome the damage done to humanity by Adam's sinful disobedience. By His single sacrificial act, Jesus has made you righteous. Righteousness isn't something achieved through our behavior—it is the result of what He has done for you and to you through His death, burial, and resurrection.

Have you believed that you can become more righteous by something you do? That is a common error. You are righteous not because of anything you do, but because of what Jesus has done. His obedience to the Father has become your obedience to Him. You are in Christ, and you stand before the Father in His righteousness, not in a self-righteousness you've gained through self-effort.

Either Jesus succeeded at the cross in providing righteousness for you, or else He failed. Will you affirm by faith that you are, at this very moment, righteous? To acknowledge your righteousness is to boast about Jesus Christ, since He is the One who is completely responsible for it.

Being Set Free

You will know the truth, and the
truth will make you free.

JOHN 8:32

One common misunderstanding about this verse has come about because people often quote only part of the verse: "The truth will make you free." What Jesus actually said is that you will *know* the truth and (then) the truth will set you free. On another occasion Jesus identified Himself as the truth. He said, "I am the way, and the truth, and the life. No one comes to the Father but through me" (John 14:6).

There are many propositional truths a person can know that will help them. But it is only by knowledge of *the* truth of Jesus Christ that we can be set free. Many immerse themselves in Bible study hoping to find freedom in the words of Scripture, but the Bible itself isn't the destination—it's a roadmap to lead us to the Destination, which is Jesus Christ.

Don't think that principles, even biblical principles, can make you free. Freedom comes when we know the Truth and trust in Him. The inspired purpose of the Bible is to reveal Him, not give a set of moral or even religious guidelines by which we are to live.

Creatures of Dust

He Himself knows our frame;
He is mindful that we are but dust.

PSALM 103:14

The tender patience of your Father toward you can be one of the most comforting aspects of your grace walk. We all tend to be hard on ourselves at times. We find ourselves disappointed that we didn't do better in a given situation. We may criticize ourselves or even feel disgust when we look at our shortcomings.

Your Father doesn't have that kind of critical attitude toward you. Jesus lived in this world as a man, and He understands what it is to live in a human body. He sits beside the right hand of His Father right now and, as a man, mediates your humanity to the Father. The wonder of that reality is that God understands.

He isn't angry toward you. He isn't impatient. He isn't frustrated because you won't get your act together. Your Father is patient and kind, tenderly working in your life to bring you to maturity. He won't give up on you but will lovingly nurture you toward becoming the person outwardly He has already made you to be on the inside. Just trust Him and show yourself plenty of grace. He does.

Personal Weakness

*God has chosen the foolish things of the world to
shame the wise, and God has chosen the weak things
of the world to shame the things which are strong.*

1 Corinthians 1:27

It's not uncommon for people to pray for God to make them stronger when they become aware of their personal weaknesses. Maybe you've prayed this prayer yourself. Perhaps you've seen strengths in others and thought that if you possessed those same strengths you could be a better person.

The irony is, sometimes it is our strengths that stand in the way of God being able to work in and through our lives to the fullest. It is often easy to depend on those strengths instead of Him. In those moments our strengths aren't an asset, but a liability to us.

The kind of person God can most readily work in and through is one who recognizes his own weakness. It is through our weakness that His strength is most readily made manifest. When we do things that we obviously couldn't have done on our own, grace shines brightly.

Don't pray for Him to make you stronger. Instead, yield your weaknesses to Him. Put them into His hands and ask Him to work through them. Then, when He does, there will be no question about who gets the glory.

Freedom from the Law

*...having canceled out the certificate of debt
consisting of decrees against us, which was
hostile to us; and He has taken it out of
the way, having nailed it to the cross.*

COLOSSIANS 2:14

You stand before God right now in a place of complete innocence. It may sound too good to be true, but the Bible explains why this is so. Under the Old Covenant, the system of Law piled one accusation after another on top of mankind because of our sin. Every person stood guilty when measured by the Old Testament Law.

When Jesus went to the cross, He took upon Himself all the guilt, the condemnation, and the consequences that the Law demanded. He bore in His body the full consequence of your sin. His vicarious death settled forever the charges the Law held against humanity.

Because of His substitutionary death, you can now rest in the fact that the decrees of the Law, which were against you and hostile toward you, have been removed and nailed to the cross. There is nothing to be held against you anymore. You owe nothing for your sin.

Don't allow yourself to feel condemned by religious rules ever again. You don't live by religious rules. Your life is found in Jesus Christ, and He has delivered you from the Law so that it can never again accuse you.

Divine Justice

The LORD longs to be gracious to you, and therefore
He waits on high to have compassion on you.
For the LORD is a God of justice;
How blessed are all those who long for Him.

ISAIAH 30:18

The justice of God is often misunderstood. Although it has often been associated with retribution, divine justice isn't about payback. Rather it is about making things right for all concerned. This verse teaches that your Lord *longs* to be gracious to you. He waits for opportune moments in your life to show you His compassion. The reason for this divine attitude is because He is a God of justice.

If you've seen God's justice as something to be feared, allow the Holy Spirit to renew your mind about the matter. He isn't watching for misbehavior so He can punish you. Your Father is watching for those perfect moments when He can pour out His grace and compassion on you to show you how much He loves you.

Don't allow fear concerning God's attitude toward you to ever find a place in your mind. He is indeed a God of justice and, because His very nature is one of love, you can long for Him at every minute of your lifetime, knowing that His only plan toward you is to express perfect love.

Negative Emotions

We will know by this that we are of the truth, and will assure our heart before Him in whatever our heart condemns us; for God is greater than our heart and knows all things. Beloved, if our heart does not condemn us, we have confidence before God.

1 JOHN 3:19-21

A condemning conscience is one of the most debilitating problems a person can have. When your conscience condemns you, you feel drained of motivation and joy in your grace walk. Using our emotions to cause us to stumble is a common strategy Satan uses against us. A condemning conscience can lead to momentary discouragement, ongoing depression, and ultimate defeat in our walk if we don't deal with it properly.

John assures us in this text that God is greater than our heart and knows all things. Your heart may tell you that you are a hypocrite when you have failed, but God knows better. It may tell you that you are a bad person, but He knows better. The emotions of your heart can deceive you if you allow it. Don't. Align your thoughts with God and find confidence to rise up and act like the person you truly are.

Ordained Days

Your eyes have seen my unformed substance;
And in Your book were all written
The days that were ordained for me,
When as yet there was not one of them.

Psalm 139:16

The details of your life don't just happen by chance. Before you were born, your heavenly Father was already intimately acquainted with you. He planned the days of your life before you breathed your first breath. Nothing that happens in your life catches the One who loves you most off guard. He sees what is going on now, and He has already orchestrated those events to work together for good in your life.

To recognize the divinely ordered structure of your lifetime can enable you to avoid needless anxiety over the temporary trials and frustrations you encounter. As you face trying moments, reaffirm the truth to yourself that everything is under control. Even when things aren't under *your* control, remember that they are all under *His* control.

To worry is to imagine a future without God in it. It is to act as if you are an orphan with nobody to care for you. Reject such lies. There is Somebody who cares for you, and He will see you through the tough times. In fact, He already has the solution worked out. You only need to walk through it by faith.

Forgiving Others

I, even I, am the one who wipes out your
transgressions for My own sake,
And I will not remember your sins.

ISAIAH 43:25

This promise about the forgiveness of sins by our God reveals much about the importance of forgiving others. The verse clearly says that God has wiped out our sins for His own sake. He has shown His grace to us by forgiving us—but that forgiveness isn't for our sake alone. It is also an expression of His nature.

God is love. For Him not to forgive our transgressions would be a contradiction within His own nature. The great love chapter in 1 Corinthians 13 reminds us that love "does not take into account a wrong suffered." God has forgiven you for His own sake—because it would be incongruent to do otherwise.

Likewise, you are now able to forgive those who have sinned against you in the same way. The source of your life is in Divine Love, so to refuse to forgive would be a contradiction of who you are at the core. You forgive others, not only for their sake, but for your own sake as well.

To refuse to forgive is to act in contradiction to your authentic self. Who do you need to forgive? Do it now by faith and in the power of divine grace.

Spiritual Anointing

You have an anointing from the
Holy One, and you all know.

1 John 2:20

Much is said in many circles about the importance of having an "anointing" on our lives. Some teach that anointing is gained through prayer. Others insist it is through the laying on of hands. Some say it comes from Bible study. The common denominator in all these teachings is the error that it comes by our own effort.

John assured those to whom He wrote that they already had an anointing. The word denotes the idea of being empowered with supernatural strength, and the apostle told them they all had such an empowering. They had it because that anointing is Christ Himself.

Jesus lives in you, and in Him you have everything you need. Later, John assures them, "As for you, the anointing which you received from Him abides in you" (1 John 2:27). "The anointing *lives* inside you," he assures them.

That same anointing lives in you. His name is Jesus Christ. You have all the supernatural power you need in Him. Don't see yourself as lacking in anything. Because you have Jesus, you have everything. Choose today to rely on that anointing to live your life in supernatural strength.

Seeing the Father

*Jesus said to him, "Have I been so long with
you, and yet you have not come to know Me,
Philip? He who has seen Me has seen the Father;
how can you say, 'Show us the Father'?"*

JOHN 14:9

Your concept of God will affect your grace walk as much as anything else in life. If you imagine Him to be distant and aloof or harsh and judgmental, you have missed the complete revelation of who He really is. If you want to know what God is like, look at Jesus.

When Philip asked to see the Father, Jesus responded by telling him that to see Him *is* to see the Father. Jesus came to reveal His Father to us and completely succeeded in doing so. He didn't reveal only one side of the Father, leaving out a dark side of His personality. Jesus showed us exactly what the Father is like.

It may be hard to reconcile some things you see in life with the portrayal of a loving Father that Jesus revealed. It may be challenging to understand some of the Old Testament scriptures about God in light of His love. One thing is certain, though: when we look at Jesus, we see the Father. So don't form your concept of God on partial information. Look at Jesus, the full revelation of the Father to us. Let your understanding of who your Father is be based on Him.

Living Free

*It was for freedom that Christ set us free;
therefore keep standing firm and do not
be subject again to a yoke of slavery.*

GALATIANS 5:1

When you have discovered your freedom in Christ and begin to walk in that freedom, don't be surprised when you encounter people who think you've "gone too far" with grace. Those whose lives are defined by religious performance don't understand how one can walk in true freedom and still live a godly lifestyle. They believe that unless we live by rules that regulate our behavior, we may become careless in how we live.

Peer pressure can be a strong influence in anybody's life. Don't give into it. Stand strong in the freedom that is your birthright in Jesus Christ. While some will criticize your freedom, others will be drawn to the truth of the gospel when they see the godly lifestyle you live with carefree abandon.

Legalistic living is slavery to dead religion. The grace walk is a lifestyle that honors God from a righteous heart, not a religious handbook somebody tries to pressure you to follow. Let Jesus be who He is in and through you. That is enough. That is the freedom He came to give you. Don't forfeit it for anybody.

Fiery Ordeals

*Beloved, do not be surprised at the fiery ordeal
among you, which comes upon you for your testing,
as though some strange thing were happening to
you; but to the degree that you share the sufferings of
Christ, keep on rejoicing, so that also at the revelation
of His glory you may rejoice with exultation.*

1 PETER 4:12-13

Faith doesn't exempt any of us from hard trials in life. Faith is the lifeline that enables us to find the strength in Christ we need. Through our faith in Christ we are able to endure the tests that come—so they prove to be productive and not destructive to our lives.

The apostle Peter told us to not be surprised when fiery ordeals come. As you face situations where the heat is turned up, you can actually find joy if you have the right perspective on the matter. It is in the midst of those trials that the presence of Christ is most visible. Peter called it "the revelation of His glory." The apostle Paul described it as "Christ in you, the hope of glory."

Severe trials in life aren't happy times. But during those times you can experience a deep joy in knowing that He is with you, and that He will lead you through your difficult time to a calmer place on the other side.

Reigning in Life

If by the transgression of the one, death reigned
through the one, much more those who receive the
abundance of grace and of the gift of righteousness
will reign in life through the One, Jesus Christ.

ROMANS 5:17

Adam's sin in the Garden of Eden had a devastating effect on all of mankind. Because of his act of disobedience, death reigned over all of humanity. However, this verse says that what Jesus accomplished was "much more" in its effect than Adam's deed. In Jesus, death is abolished and we are able to reign in a righteous life by grace.

God's grace has been given to you in abundance, and His righteousness is yours as a gift. Your potential to live a greater life than you can imagine is yours simply by receiving these two gifts by faith.

You are destined to live above mediocrity. You have been created to reign in life—to live miraculously. As you accept His grace and believe the truth about your own righteous identity in Him, you will be amazed by how He works in the circumstances of your daily life. The possibility to reign is exponentially greater in Christ than the depths of ruin you would have experienced in Adam. Receive His grace. Appropriate His righteousness as your own and reign!

No Remembering Sins

*I will be merciful to their iniquities, and
I will remember their sins no more.*

HEBREWS 8:12

The promise that God will not remember our sins anymore doesn't mean that He forgets. The assurance is much greater than that. To refuse to remember our sins shows how merciful our Father is toward us.

Consider this example: Your finger is a member on your hand. If you were to accidentally cut off your finger, it is possible that somebody could pick it up, pack it in ice, and rush you to the hospital with your severed finger. You would most likely be rushed into surgery, where the surgeon would seek to "re-member" your finger by reattaching it to your hand.

That's the meaning of the word as used in this verse. You can be confident that your sins have been severed from you through the finished work of Christ on the cross. They will never be "remembered" again. Your sins are gone, and you have the personal commitment from God that He will never remember them again.

Walk into this day in the joy of knowing your sins will never be remembered!

Courage in Troubles

These things I have spoken to you, so that in Me you may have peace. In the world you have tribulation, but take courage; I have overcome the world.

<small>JOHN 16:33</small>

There is no exemption for us when it comes to experiencing troubles in this life. In fact, Jesus told us that we would have tribulation. This world is an environment in which trials and troubles are an intrinsic part. No amount of faith can change that fact.

The good news is that we aren't left alone in our tribulations. Jesus is our peace and gives us good reason to take courage. He has overcome the world. That guarantees we won't be overcome by life's circumstances.

Whatever tribulations you may face, keep your eyes on Him. The ups and downs of life's details can toss your emotions around like a cork on the surf. His indwelling life can stabilize your emotions and settle your frenzied thoughts. Choose to focus on what you know—that your Father is good and that the Spirit of Jesus is in you to walk through your situation with you. Don't focus on what you don't know, allowing your imagination to run wild about the future. The One who has overcome the world is in control and He loves you.

A Motherly God

You will be nursed; you will be carried on the
hip and fondled on the knees. As one whom
his mother comforts, so I will comfort you;
and you will be comforted in Jerusalem.

ISAIAH 66:12-13

Think about times you've been in public and seen a misbehaving young toddler. He may be running around a store reaching for everything he shouldn't touch. It's not uncommon to see his mother reach down and pick him up, perch him on her hip, and carry him.

Or think of times you've been at a solemn event such as a wedding or funeral. A young child begins to be restless and making noise. The mother will often take that child on her lap and gently stroke him until his restlessness gives way to the comfort that leads to sleep on her bosom.

Our God's behavior is the same way toward us. When you misbehave, the response isn't one of divine impatience. Your God gently picks you up and carries you to keep you from getting into trouble or hurting yourself.

When you are restless, God holds you close and gently strokes your heart with love until you find peace and renewed rest. Don't ever doubt His love. You'll be carried, caressed, and loved for all eternity, no matter what you may be doing or not doing.

God Is for You

This I know, that God is for me.

PSALM 56:9

Have you ever found yourself in a place where it seems like life is against you? Sometimes it seems like nothing works in our favor. In those moments, we may be tempted to wonder where God is in all that's going on.

The answer is simple. He is with you. Not only is He with you, but God is for you. This is a fact you need to settle in your mind once and for all time. Unless you have established firmly in your heart and mind that God is for you, you will be an easy target for attack every time things seem to go wrong.

When we can't see the hand of God at work in our circumstances, then we have the opportunity to exercise our faith. There is no room for faith when there is no room for doubt. So the fact that the situation seems to suggest your Father isn't involved makes it a perfect time for declaring in faith and faith alone, "This I know, that God is *for* me!"

Friends with Christ

*No longer do I call you slaves, for the slave does
not know what his master is doing; but I have
called you friends, for all things that I have heard
from My Father I have made known to you.*

JOHN 15:15

Understanding the difference between being a servant and being a friend of Jesus will make a huge difference in how you experience your grace walk. One creates a heavy sense of duty, and the other gives life to the experience of joyful delight.

Slaves do what they do because they don't want to make their master angry. Friends do things for each other because they love each other and want to make the other happy because of love. Slaves do the bare minimum to satisfy the boss. Friends go overboard so they can thrill the heart of their companion. Slaves try to keep the rules. Friends don't live by rules but are motivated by the relationship they have with the one they love.

Do you behave in your relationship to Christ like a slave or a friend? The fact is that He adores you and always will, no matter what you do or how well you do it. Ask Him to help you grow in friendship with Him. As you do, you'll find your motivation becoming an increasingly joyful one.

Sin-Consciousness

The Law, since it has only a shadow of the good things
to come and not the very form of things, can never,
by the same sacrifices which they offer continually
year by year, make perfect those who draw near.
Otherwise, would they not have ceased to be offered,
because the worshipers, having once been cleansed,
would no longer have had consciousness of sins?

HEBREWS 10:1-2

The sacrifices of the Old Testament served as a reminder to the people of the sins they had committed. The reason the sacrifices were repeated every year is because they were imperfect. They could cover only the sins of the previous year. Had a sacrifice been perfect, it could have taken away all the people's sins, and they would have lost their consciousness of them.

When Jesus offered Himself, He was the perfect sacrifice. He did what bulls and goats could never do under the Old Covenant. He took away *all* your sins. He didn't just cover them, but removed them from you forever.

Because of His perfect work, you never have to be sin-conscious again. The biblical text above clearly shows that sin-consciousness is a sign of the Old Covenant of Law. You are under a New Covenant now. You are free to be Christ-conscious and to set aside all preoccupation with sin. It's gone. Forget it and focus on Jesus alone.

Heartfelt Obedience

*Thanks be to God that though you were slaves of
sin, you became obedient from the heart to that
form of teaching to which you were committed.*

ROMANS 6:17

You are not a slave to sin. It has absolutely no power
over you. Its only ability is to deceive you into believing that you're helpless when tempted. But you aren't.
Jesus Christ is your life. You are defined by His love and
life, which indwell you.

As you continue to be set free from the old legalistic teachings that held you in a place where you thought
you had to fight to overcome temptations, you will
increasingly learn that you are actually free to live from
your heart. When you know that your heart's desire is
to glorify God through your actions, obedience to Him
isn't a burden but is a blessing.

Affirm right now that your heart's desire is toward
Him. Despite sin's momentary magnetism, your default
setting is to hate it. See that reality. Recognize the heartfelt love for Christ that lies within you and live from
that place. You'll discover that the struggle will stop and
you will be able to live from the overflow of love.

No More Rules

You also were made to die to the Law through the body of Christ, so that you might be joined to another, to Him who was raised from the dead, in order that we might bear fruit for God.

ROMANS 7:4

The Law is a system of religious rules found in the Old Testament. You don't live under a law system anymore. Not only are you free from the Laws of the Old Testament, but you are even free from contemporary religious rules. You have no relationship to that lifestyle whatsoever.

You were crucified with Jesus and have died to any and every rules-keeping system. You don't need rules! You have been joined in union with Jesus Christ so that His life and yours are one.

As you recognize Him to be your Life-Source and as you trust Him moment by moment, you will bear fruit in your life that glorifies God in a wonderful way. It won't be something you have to make happen. It will be the normal result of Christ expressing Himself through you.

Renew your mind to the fact that you don't need rules. You have Jesus. His life is what controls your behavior. Look to Him and never look back on religious rules again.

Thinking the Right Way

*If you have been raised up with Christ, keep seeking
the things above, where Christ is, seated at the right
hand of God. Set your mind on the things above,
not on the things that are on earth. For you have
died and your life is hidden with Christ in God.*

COLOSSIANS 3:1-3

What you think about has a huge effect on your life. Put your mind in the wrong place, and it will affect your whole day in a negative way. Learn to set your mind in the right place, and you'll be amazed by how it changes your outlook no matter what the day may bring.

You have been raised up with Jesus Christ. You are a new person who is in Him to the extent that His life is yours. So don't allow your mind to get bogged down in the muck and mire of superficial things. See everything through a supernatural lens.

Paul said to direct your mental and emotional energy toward the things that are above, where Christ is. You are in Him, and He is seated by the right hand of the Father. You never need to live "under the circumstances" again. Your life is hidden with Christ in God!

Endless Kindness

The LORD's lovingkindnesses indeed never cease,
For His compassions never fail.
They are new every morning;
Great is Your faithfulness.

LAMENTATIONS 3:22-23

Sometimes the circumstances of life wear us out physically, emotionally, and mentally. In those moments it becomes easy to develop a victim mentality. We begin to think that every day is a dead-end repeat of the day before, and it seems like we're on a treadmill, with little hope for change.

The promise above from Lamentations is an oasis of hope on days like that. The Bible promises that our Lord's lovingkindnesses never cease. God never runs out of goodness when it comes to you! His heart of compassion toward you will never be empty! Regardless of how you may feel, your God is never, never, never going to stop renewing you with His strength and goodness.

Every day of your life you will find that your faithful God is there to uphold you. In Jesus Christ, you are a victor! Rise up and face the circumstances of your life in the assurance that God will work in them to accomplish something good. Trust in His faithfulness and bet your life on His goodness. You have a divine guarantee that you will not be disappointed in the end.

A New Heart

I will give you a new heart and put a new spirit within you; and I will remove the heart of stone from your flesh and give you a heart of flesh.

Ezekiel 36:26

Don't ever allow yourself to believe that you're a bad person. Even when you have done something that tempts you to see yourself as bad, remember that you are not defined by what you do. The One who lives in you determines your true identity. Don't believe anything to the contrary.

It may be tempting at times to stare at your failures, your weaknesses, and the areas of your life where you believe you are deficient. It's tempting to conclude that you aren't all you ought to be. Do not travel that legalistic pathway. It will only lead to self-condemnation and defeat.

At the core of your being, you are a righteous child of God. You have been given a new heart. Maybe you've focused on the Old Testament verse that talks about the heart being deceitful and desperately wicked. However, you don't live in the Old Testament. You live in New Covenant times, and things have changed.

Your heart is new because a new Spirit—His Spirit—lives in you. So reject lies that come to your mind and walk in the truth of your new heart.

A Real Disciple

*By this all men will know that you are My
disciples, if you have love for one another.*

John 13:35

There are many aspects of our faith that people believe
are primary. Some think that correct doctrine is most
important. Others believe that worship is the foundation of our lifestyle. Some would argue that evangelism
is the key to being a disciple of Jesus. Take a poll and
there will be a multitude of opinions.

Jesus narrowed it all down to the one thing that
identifies His disciples. He said that love is the main
thing. We might know sound doctrine and even be able
to teach it, but if people don't see us as loving, what
good is our knowledge? We can follow a biblical pattern of worship that angels would admire, but if people
don't know we love them, what good is it? We can proclaim the gospel to everybody in our town, but if they
don't sense love, what result can we expect?

Love is everything. God is love, and if we aren't
expressing love to everybody we meet, we aren't expressing Him to them. Apart from love, anything we do is
nothing more than dead, religious activity.

Look around today and find somebody you can
truly show the love of God. When you do that, you're
behaving like a real disciple.

Bearing Fruit

*Abide in Me, and I in you. As the branch
cannot bear fruit of itself unless it abides in
the vine, so neither can you unless you abide
in Me. I am the vine, you are the branches; he
who abides in Me and I in him, he bears much
fruit, for apart from Me you can do nothing.*

JOHN 15:4-5

The battle cry of religion is that we are to do something for God. "Let's do something great for God!" and other such mottos fill churches across the world. The emphasis sounds noble—but in reality it's as far from a biblical pattern as we could get.

Jesus said that there is nothing we can do for Him. We can't produce fruit any more than a grape could suddenly appear before us. Fruit is the result of life flowing from the vine through the branch to which it is connected. The branch *bears* the fruit but it doesn't produce it. The vine does.

Rather than focusing on doing something for God, you (and He) will be much better served if you focus on *Him*. It is out of our intimate union with Christ that godly and lasting fruit is produced.

Learn to rest in His life within you, allowing Him to animate your actions, and fruit will be the result. Try to do something for Him and all you can do will add up to zero.

Quality of Life

Come to Me, all who are weary and heavy-laden,
and I will give you rest. Take My yoke upon you
and learn from Me, for I am gentle and humble
in heart, and you will find rest for your souls.
For My yoke is easy and My burden is light.

MATTHEW 11:28-30

Ask the average person to describe his or her life in three words and you will probably hear words like "busy, stressful, demanding," or other adjectives that reveal the trend of modern culture. The description would probably stand in stark contradiction to the kind of life Jesus offers. The life He invites us to participate in is one of "rest." He uses the words "easy" to describe His yoke and "light" to describe His burden.

What adjectives would you use to describe your life right now? If they aren't the same words Jesus would use, you might ask yourself if you are enjoying the life that is yours for the taking in Him.

Ask Him to show you if you need to take a new approach to how you live your daily life. Is it possible that some things aren't as important as you've thought?

Living Water

He who believes in Me, as the Scripture said, "From his innermost being will flow rivers of living water."

JOHN 7:38

There is a vast difference between living in "the Christian religion" and living a biblical Christian lifestyle. The Christian religion could be compared to a reservoir where water is stored and dispensed as deemed necessary. An authentic grace walk is a biblical lifestyle in which the living water of Christ's life flows from within us. It doesn't have to be dispensed sparingly or pumped up. It flows out under its own power as it overflows from our lives into the lives of others.

Religious institutions are often formed around programs designed to dispense their message. But when the members of the church of Jesus Christ become caught up in His life and love, He—the one who is *the message*—comes spontaneously gushing out of us, soaking everybody in our path with the love of the Father. It isn't so much a decision to "be a witness" as it is a supernatural outflow of a Life too big and too wonderful to contain.

If you happen to find yourself in the religious reservoir, break free by realizing that the righteous river of life within you will effortlessly flow from you as you trust in Christ. Organizations are fine as long as they aren't only organizations but are also organisms teeming with Divine Life.

Drawing Near

Let us draw near with confidence to the
throne of grace, so that we may receive mercy
and find grace to help in time of need.

HEBREWS 4:16

Be careful to never confuse humility with a religious inferiority complex. Humility exists when we see ourselves as our Father sees us—no more and no less. A religious inferiority complex causes us to look down on ourselves and believe that we aren't worthy to approach our Father with boldness.

This verse from Hebrews directs us to draw near to the throne of grace with confidence. You don't have to be timid when you pray. You are worthy because Jesus Christ has made you worthy. You are a child of God. He delights in you when you approach Him in complete transparency and totally without inhibition.

Your God is your *Abba*—your Daddy. Approach Him with the eager expectation of childlike faith, knowing that you will most certainly receive His mercy and find grace to help in every need you have.

Made Holy

A voice came to him a second time, "What God
has cleansed, no longer consider unholy."

ACTS 10:15

In Acts 10, Peter had a vision about animals descending from heaven on a sheet. There were all kinds of animals, both clean and unclean according to the Law. When God told him to eat, he resisted by reminding Him that no good Jew would eat an unclean animal. It was at that point that God spoke these words to him: "What God has cleansed, no longer consider unholy."

The lesson Peter needed to learn wasn't one primarily about animals, but about people. God was about to send him to the house of Cornelius, a Gentile who Peter would have considered unholy up till then.

Are you holy? How you answer that question says much about your own perspective on this matter. By His blood, Jesus has cleansed you. By His grace, He has made you holy. To grow in your grace walk, it is important to affirm that fact. Don't deny or even diminish the reality that you are holy. You didn't do anything to make it happen. He did—so simply thank and praise Him for it. And, as God taught Peter, it would be wise to see other believers in that light too.

Looking at the Eternal

…we look not at the things which are seen,
but at the things which are not seen; for the
things which are seen are temporal, but the
things which are not seen are eternal.

2 Corinthians 4:18

The gravitational pull on our attention by the temporal things of this world sometimes seems almost irresistible. It takes deliberate intention to look beyond the superficial things to the unseen foundation that rests in those things that are eternal.

As you experience the frustrations of daily living, choose to look beyond the immediate circumstances toward the underlying reality that your life is in Christ and He is securely planted in His Father. The Spirit keeps you there.

It may seem hard to see that reality when the pressures of the day close in on you, but the Bible doesn't say to *see* it. It simply says to *look* at the things that aren't seen. What a paradox! Look at what you can't see? That's right. The only way it can be done is to look by faith at what you know is true. Even if you can't see, look. By looking to the Eternal One, you have acted in faith and risen above the situation at hand.

Biblical Verification

*These were more noble-minded than those
in Thessalonica, for they received the word
with great eagerness, examining the Scriptures
daily to see whether these things were so.*

ACTS 17:11

The Berean Christians were commended by Paul for not only enthusiastically receiving the word, but also for examining the Scripture for themselves to see whether or not his message was true. Their example still stands as a pattern for "noble-minded" people.

There are two extremes in the modern church. There are those who believe everything they hear. And there are those who don't believe anything they hear unless they already have heard and come to believe it. Both extremes are a mistake.

When you hear a teaching that is unfamiliar to you and you aren't sure what to think, don't immediately accept or reject it based on your present understanding. Go to the Scriptures for yourself and study to see whether the things you have heard are so.

The Spirit of Christ lives in you and will guide you into the truth if your heart and mind are open to Him. Believe what the Holy Spirit shows you, and the truth becomes yours. Otherwise the most you can do is to parrot what somebody else has said. As one in whom Truth lives, you are capable of much more than that.

Grace, Our Teacher

*The grace of God has appeared, bringing
salvation to all men, instructing us to deny
ungodliness and worldly desires and to live
sensibly, righteously and godly in the present age.*

TITUS 2:11-12

The fear that teaching grace will cause people to become careless in their walk is unfounded. Understanding the grace of God never causes anybody to take sin lightly. To the contrary, grace takes a person's focus off sin altogether and draws his or her attention and energy to living a godly lifestyle.

Grace is a teacher because grace is a Person. The Spirit of Jesus is the Spirit of Grace, who instructs and inspires you to live the kind of lifestyle that honors God in this world. Grace creates godly desires within you and empowers you to see those desires realized.

Anybody who warns that you had better be careful about grace teaching hasn't understood the authentic grace of the Father expressed through His Son by the Spirit. You don't have to worry about grace leading you to go astray in your grace walk. It will have the exact opposite effect.

Personal Ability

The LORD said to him, "What is that in your hand?"
And he said, "A staff." Then He said, "Throw it on
the ground." So he threw it on the ground, and it
became a serpent; and Moses fled from it. But the
LORD said to Moses, "Stretch out your hand and grasp
it by its tail"—so he stretched out his hand and
caught it, and it became a staff in his hand.

EXODUS 4:2-4

When God sent Moses into the desert, he lost everything he had known. The only way he still provided for himself was as a shepherd. It was his last thin strand of self-sufficiency. His shepherd's staff represented his ability to survive, even in the hardest of times.

So God did what He always does when He wants to work through a person's life in a miraculous way. He had Moses throw his staff down. We cannot rely on our own ability if we are to fulfill our divine destiny in life.

When Moses threw the staff down, it became a snake. Dependence on our ability instead of God is always poisonous. However, once Moses saw that fact, God told him to pick the staff back up. It's not the ability itself that is wrong. Our mistake comes when we don't depend on God.

God will use your ability for His glory, but never forget that it is He—not the ability you possess—who equips you.

An Eternal Home

The eternal God is a dwelling place, and
underneath are the everlasting arms.

DEUTERONOMY 33:27

You were created to live as an eternal being with your Father in heaven. This world is a temporary place to live. It's a neighborhood you won't be in forever. Your home is in God. He is your lasting dwelling place.

A man once told me about living in a dangerous, run-down neighborhood on the mission field. It was a harsh environment, even dangerous at times. "My home is like an oasis there," he said. "When I go inside to my loving wife and family, I feel loved and at rest."

That's a picture of what it means to know God as your dwelling place. The world outside may be hostile, even threatening at times. But as you recognize that your life is in Him, you can find peace, love, and security.

You stand in a secure place with your God as your dwelling place. His everlasting arms will hold you, protect you, and hug you in every situation. Face each day with the confidence that your God holds you in His arms. Live boldly with the knowledge that you cannot be conquered by the world around you, because you belong to Him.

Blessed with Everything

Blessed be the God and Father of our Lord Jesus Christ, who has blessed us with every spiritual blessing in the heavenly places in Christ.

EPHESIANS 1:3

Living out of a perspective of lack will keep you from experiencing the benefits that are inherent to your grace walk. Don't think for a moment that you lack anything you need. God has blessed you with every spiritual blessing in Christ. There is no shortage in the kingdom of God.

Contemporary Christianity often misleads people by instructing them to long for holiness, to push for breakthroughs, to pray for divine power. Or it challenges them in other ways that imply we lack something that can be gained if we just know and follow the right formula.

You don't lack anything. You *are* holy. Jesus has already made the breakthrough for you. You have the divine power of His life within you.

You can probably think of areas in your own life where you have felt a sense of lack. Renounce those thoughts. When you received Christ, you received all you need. Everything you need is yours in Him, and every blessing is a spiritual blessing because it comes from your heavenly Father. Look to Him and never see yourself as lacking anything again.

The Desires of Your Heart

Delight yourself in the LORD;
And He will give you the desires of your heart.

PSALM 37:4

Sometimes you may wonder if the things you want are desires that your Father wants to fulfill or if they are selfish desires. This verse gives assurance that if you delight in the Lord, He will give you the desires of your heart. Does that mean that God is like a cosmic Santa Claus, who will give us a Rolls-Royce and a mansion with a Jacuzzi simply because we want them?

The key to the meaning of this verse is to understand that God doesn't simply give us what we desire. He is the one who places our desires within us as we delight ourselves in Him. In other words, He causes us to want what He wants us to want. And then He gives us those things.

Focus on Him, and then trust Him to put the desires in you that are right for you. Don't overanalyze your motives. Just put your desires in His hands and know that He will deal with them in His way and timing.

A Precious Treasure

*The kingdom of heaven is like a treasure
hidden in the field, which a man found and
hid again; and from joy over it he goes and
sells all that he has and buys that field.*

MATTHEW 13:44

Religious thought often seeks to make man the hero
in the parables of Jesus. This parable is a good example.
You've probably heard it said that the treasure hidden in
the field is Jesus and we should be willing to give anything to know Him. However, that's not what the parable is teaching.

Is it really possible that we could "buy" Jesus as the
man in this parable buys the hidden treasure? No, the
Hero of this story is Jesus Christ. You didn't buy Him.
He bought you. He saw you in this world (the field) and
gave all that He had (His life) for the world so you
might belong to Him. You have been bought with a
price and it was a great price, but you were worth it
to Him.

See yourself as treasured by Christ and you will discover joy rising up in you. You are a precious treasure to
God. That is your true identity. Claim it as being true
and praise Him for it.

Serving Others

Have this attitude in yourselves which was also in Christ Jesus, who, although He existed in the form of God, did not regard equality with God a thing to be grasped, but emptied Himself, taking the form of a bond-servant, and being made in the likeness of men.

PHILIPPIANS 2:5-7

Jesus was willing to lay aside the privileges of Deity in heaven and come to earth as a human being in order to bring you back to the Father. He emptied Himself of divine prerogatives and became a servant for our sake.

Jesus was fully God and fully man, but He never once used His divine power for selfish ends. Every time He demonstrated His miraculous power it was for the benefit of others. The King of kings came to earth to serve.

Never allow pride to become an obstacle when it comes to serving others. When you humble yourself and demonstrate love in action toward those who have no way to repay you and nothing to offer in return, take joy in knowing that you are expressing the love of Jesus to them. That kind of service expresses greatness in eternity.

Rejoice in the Lord

*Finally, my brethren, rejoice in the Lord. To
write the same things again is no trouble
to me, and it is a safeguard for you.*

PHILIPPIANS 3:1

These words of the apostle Paul weren't written from
the lap of luxury but were penned from a jail cell. Paul
had learned the secret of joy to the extent that his circumstances had no power to steal it. He had discovered that joy is "in the Lord." Nobody would want to
be imprisoned—but Paul had realized that jail was only
temporary and Jesus is forever.

When you find yourself in situations that threaten
to steal your joy, look beyond the momentary trial you
face. Recognize that the source of your well-being isn't
in a place or a predicament but in the Person who is
with you in that very moment.

In difficult circumstances, perspective is everything.
You can focus on the superficial details of the moment,
or you can plumb the depths of God's love for you as
you endure the hard times. There is something about
troubles that strips away the temporary things of life
and allows us to see Jesus more clearly. Choose a perspective that sees Him, and live above your circumstances.

Holy Pleasure

*You shall eat in the presence of the LORD your
God, at the place where He chooses to establish His
name, the tithe of your grain, your new wine, your
oil, and the firstborn of your herd and your flock,
so that you may learn to fear the LORD your God
always... You may spend the money for whatever
your heart desires: for oxen, or sheep, or wine, or
strong drink, or whatever your heart desires; and
there you shall eat in the presence of the LORD
your God and rejoice, you and your household.*

DEUTERONOMY 14:23,26

In this passage God instructed His people to enjoy life
to the fullest so that they might learn to fear Him. What
a wonderful way for Him to teach how much He loved
them! It's difficult to read this passage and not conclude
that our God takes delight in our pleasure. He isn't a cosmic
killjoy—He is the source and origin of pleasure itself.

Never allow the idea to take root in your mind
that your Father is opposed to playfulness and pleasure.
Satan may have corrupted those domains, but those
who know the Lord need to reclaim these as rightful
privileges of the children of the King.

Honor your God today by celebrating with others.
Laugh, love, and learn that deep reverence toward Him
comes from realizing that He delights to see us at play.

Sin's Consequence

The LORD God commanded the man, saying,
"From any tree of the garden you may eat
freely; but from the tree of the knowledge of
good and evil you shall not eat, for in the day
that you eat from it you will surely die."

GENESIS 2:16-17

The grace of God can be seen in the Garden of Eden when He warned Adam not to eat from the tree of the knowledge of good and evil. God cautioned Adam that he would die if he ate from that tree. Notice that God did not tell Adam that He would kill him if he ate from the tree. The prohibition was given in love, not as a threat.

Over the millennia many have misunderstood this text. They have seen it as a warning from God about what He would do if man sinned. Nothing could be further from the truth. God warned man about what *sin* would do to him if he submitted to it.

Your Father isn't out to get you when you sin. He has given warnings in the Bible about sin and its consequences, but remember this: it is sin that punishes, not God. To the contrary, when Adam sinned and hid from his God, the Father came to him to rescue him. He does the same for you. Never think otherwise.

God Isn't Hungry

If I were hungry I would not tell you,
For the world is Mine, and all it contains.

The world of religion puts such an emphasis on what we are to do for God. This mistaken emphasis isn't benign, because it gives people the impression that there really is something we could do for God. That false understanding easily leads to the notion that He needs us to do His work.

God doesn't need anything. With divine wit, He spoke through the psalmist, "If I were hungry I wouldn't tell you." God has everything that He needs. Our service is His way of allowing us to participate in what He is doing in this world. He certainly could do it without us.

Renounce the idea that God is expecting you to do something for Him. Replace that faulty view with the truth that He *allows* you to join Him in what He's doing in this world. God doesn't need you, but the beauty of grace is that He enjoys it when you partner together with Him in what He is doing in this world. Gain that perspective and you'll find that service becomes a real joy.

Sin Is Destroyed

...He has been manifested to put away
sin by the sacrifice of Himself.

HEBREWS 9:26

Before the first atom was created, our Triune God already had the provision for sin settled. There was no way He was going to leave humanity in the grip of Adam's sin, being destroyed by its power. His love was the catalyst that caused Him to become a man and defeat sin as a human.

This verse says that Christ was manifested to "put away sin." The phrase denotes the idea of disannulling it completely. The root word suggests the idea of "making void, to nullify, to thwart its efficacy." In other words, Jesus didn't just put a Band-Aid on sin. He removed it and completely disarmed its power over mankind.

You don't have to struggle with sin anymore. You don't have to feel guilty about sins ever again. Jesus has dealt with sin quite effectively. He dealt with every sin of your lifetime before you were even born. He took your sin into Himself and by His own sacrifice destroyed its power, leaving you completely free from its eternal penalty. Trust in what He has done and don't even allow sin to find a place in your mind.

Severe Trials

*We do not have a high priest who cannot sympathize
with our weaknesses, but One who has been
tempted in all things as we are, yet without sin.*

HEBREWS 4:15

When you find yourself in the middle of a situation where your faith is being tested to the limit, sometimes the negative feelings become so acute that you wonder if God really cares. It can seem at times like nobody understands. Those feelings of isolation and helplessness can lead to despair.

The reality is that you are never alone in your trials. When you are tempted to give in to hopelessness, that is the time to exercise faith by reminding yourself of the truth. You are not alone. Jesus knows how you feel because He too faced every sort of trial common to us.

In the midst of confusion, questions, and pain, pause and set your mind on the truth. Close your eyes and, through the eyes of faith, see Him holding you. He whispers assurance to you that He knows exactly how you feel and that He will bring you through this trial. Then, believe Him…because it's true.

Deliverance from Sins

He will again have compassion on us;
He will tread our iniquities under foot.
Yes, You will cast all their sins
into the depths of the sea.

Micah 7:19

When it seems that your failures, even your sinful actions, have the upper hand in your life, it becomes easy to get discouraged. It may feel like your Father is a long way from you in those moments. It is in those moments that you need to remind yourself of the truth.

"He will again have compassion on us." Your Father never becomes exasperated with you. His love for you is the cause for unending patience and continuous compassion. You are His precious child, and when he sees you in danger of being hurt by a sinful deed, He stands ready to rush to your assistance.

Like a natural father would rush toward his little child who was about to pick up a poisonous snake, your heavenly Father rushes to you when you're on the brink of disaster. Look to Him and He will "tread [your] iniquities under foot." His heart toward you is never to shame or punish you, but to deliver you from the sin that would destroy you.

Call out to Him in times of temptation. Run to Him when you feel overcome by your own failures. His compassion will make things right.

The Divine Nature

He has granted to us His precious and magnificent
promises, so that by them you may become
partakers of the divine nature, having escaped
the corruption that is in the world by lust.

2 PETER 1:4

The single greatest aspect of what Christ has done in you through His finished work on the cross is this: He has made you a partaker of the divine nature. You have divine life pulsating through the core of your being. Understanding your union with God is the most transforming truth you will ever know in this world.

The Father, Son, and Holy Spirit have lived in a circle of harmony and love for all eternity. Through Jesus you have been brought into that circle. The Adamic nature is dead, and you now possess the divine nature of your Creator. His life defines your very being.

Go forward in your grace walk with the understanding of your true identity. You aren't trying to achieve something spiritually. You aren't trying to make progress with God in any way. Jesus Christ has finished that work, and now you find your existence within the Trinity. The knowledge of this reality has inestimable ability to transform the way you live your life each day.

People-Pleasers

*Am I now seeking the favor of men, or of God? Or
am I striving to please men? If I were still trying to
please men, I would not be a bond-servant of Christ.*

GALATIANS 1:10

The apostle Paul was constantly criticized for his message of grace. The religious community of his day thought that his message was heresy. They accused him of being soft on sin, of disrespecting sacred traditions, and of departing from sound doctrine. He was accused of saying what people wanted to hear instead of teaching pure truth—of being a people-pleaser.

The same thing happens today when you stand for the biblical message of grace. The irony is that those who accuse you of saying what people want to hear are the very ones who don't want to hear it! Pure grace angers the religionists because it takes all the glory away from them and what they do—and gives all the credit to Jesus Christ.

Don't back down when you are criticized for your grace walk. Stand firm and boldly live the life you have been given in Christ. You aren't alone. Paul was criticized too. So know you are in good company.

Divine Faithfulness

If we are faithless, He remains faithful,
for He cannot deny Himself.

2 TIMOTHY 2:13

Nothing brings a greater experience of spiritual rest than knowing that our acceptance by our God is based on His faithfulness and not our own. The Father, Son, and Holy Spirit have entered into an eternal agreement together concerning you. In Christ your security has been established forever. It isn't because of what you may do or not do, but because of what He has done.

Until we realize the faithfulness of God toward us, our focus will invariably be on our own performance. We will wonder if our faithfulness is consistent enough, strong enough, and sincere enough to relax in the Father's acceptance. Once we realize that His faithfulness never changes even when our faithfulness falters, we will be able to enjoy the spiritual rest known only by those who truly understand His grace.

Meditate on the faithfulness of God toward you, and you will be released from having to examine your own faithfulness toward Him. The power of grace is that, once you fully believe in His faithfulness, your own will increase exponentially.

Entering Canaan

*Moses My servant is dead; now therefore arise, cross
this Jordan, you and all this people, to the land
which I am giving to them, to the sons of Israel.*

JOSHUA 1:2

Moses wasn't able to lead Israel into Canaan. It took
Joshua to do that. This isn't an incidental matter. Moses
is remembered primarily as the one who brought God's
Law to the people. The name "Joshua" is the Hebrew
equivalent of the name "Jesus."

When God told Joshua that Moses was dead and
that he was to lead the people across the Jordan into
Canaan, His instructions convey an important message
for us today. We will never experience the abundant
life our Father wants us to know by following religious
rules. Moses, who represents the rules-keeping system,
is dead to us and us to him. Our leader is Joshua (Jesus).
He alone is our guide into the awesome life God has
given us.

Moses is dead. Don't try to build your lifestyle
around religious rules. The grace walk is a journey with
Jesus. He will lead you from a lifestyle of struggling to
get to where you want to be to the place of entering in
by faith in Him alone.

Righteous by Grace

He made Him who knew no sin to be sin
on our behalf, so that we might become
the righteousness of God in Him.

2 Corinthians 5:21

Jesus took your sin into Himself so that you could take His righteousness as your own. You are a righteous person. It isn't because you behave a particular way or even because you believe a particular thing. It's because of what Jesus has done on your behalf. He has made you righteous by exchanging your life for His.

Maybe you have thought that you could become righteous by overcoming sins and doing the things you believed would please God. The good news of the gospel is that your righteousness has nothing to do with your actions—it is 100 percent the result of His act on the cross.

Exercise faith in this finished work of Christ right now by affirming that you are the righteousness of God because of Jesus. Don't misjudge your true identity because you don't feel righteous or because you don't act that way at times.

To benefit from what Jesus has done, you may need to change your thinking about this subject. Jesus Christ has made you righteous. Believe it and then live as if it's true, because it is.

Living Boldly

The wicked flee when no one is pursuing,
But the righteous are bold as a lion.

PROVERBS 28:1

There is no reason to be paranoid or even tentative about living each day with boldness. You are a righteous person who possesses the life of Jesus Christ. Your success is as certain as His commitment to you. Don't worry about the outcome of your endeavors—instead, be focused on moving through the process in the power of His indwelling Spirit. It isn't the destination that requires faith. It's the daily journey toward it that calls for trust in Him.

When a person doesn't know or believe that Christ expresses Himself through him or her, there's a legitimate reason to be afraid. If you were the guarantor of your future, the future would be uncertain at best. But your future is in the hands of the One who guides you with every step you take. So don't be afraid. Trust that He has set your course, and move onward.

When Jesus Christ is guiding your steps you cannot fail! Regardless of the outcome, He *is* your success in life. For that reason, don't be timid about life. Live boldly in the confidence that He is in full control.

Victory Always

*Thanks be to God, who always leads
us in triumph in Christ.*

2 Corinthians 2:14

The Bible says that your Father always causes you to triumph in Christ. Either it is true that you *always* triumph, or it isn't. The Scripture isn't ambiguous on this subject. If you assume the identity of "failure" when you don't achieve the outcome you hoped for, you are setting yourself up for a chronic deception and, consequently, continuous defeat. Your success rests in the fact that Jesus Christ is the source of your life. You will never *be* a failure because Divine DNA flows from your spirit.

Armed with the knowledge that you can't be a failure, you are in the unique position of being able to attempt great things. If you truly believed you could never be a failure, what would you attempt? The apostle Paul wrote, "I can do all things through Christ who strengthens me." The same is true of you.

Does that mean that things will always turn out exactly the way you want? No. What it does mean is that no matter what the result is, you can move forward knowing that no temporary failure defines who you are. In fact, it is often true that apparent failures are not *actual* failures. They may actually be tools in the hands of God intended to teach us, strengthen us, and guide us into His perfect plan.

Overcoming Fear

*I was with you in weakness and in
fear and in much trembling.*

1 CORINTHIANS 2:3

When Paul faced the daunting assignment to go to Corinth and establish a church, he felt fear, but he acted anyway. Courage is acting boldly in the face of fear. That's what Paul did. He faced his fears and then *acted* bravely.

Our greatest threat is not fear. The greatest threat is inactivity *because of* fear. You *will* feel fear at times. The question is, will you face your fears and move through them, trusting God as you go forward with knocking knees or a nervous stomach?

When Jesus was in the Garden of Gethsemane on the night before His crucifixion, surely He experienced feelings of fear. What else would have caused Him to sweat blood and ask His Father if there was any way for Him to take away what was to come?

He faced His fears, then *acted in faith*. He didn't succumb to them. He refused to give in to those feelings and instead moved forward with faith in His Father. He will empower you now to do the same.

Don't wait until you feel no fear to move ahead, or it will never happen. Every new endeavor offers some reason to be afraid. If you wait until you feel courageous, you may never act. Trust Him and move ahead.

Heavenly Assignments

I have accomplished the work which
You have given me to do.

JESUS, IN JOHN 17:4

The grace walk isn't a passive lifestyle. In the final hours before His crucifixion, Jesus prayed to the Father and acknowledged that He had accomplished the work He had been given to do.

You have an opportunity to fulfill a divine mission too. The sultry sirens of the status quo beckon us all to lie back and be passive. The call to those who want to live a grace-empowered lifestyle is to rise up in the power of the Life that indwells them. Take chances, knowing that your Father guides you in every thought and action as you depend upon Him.

It isn't your responsibility to make sure that things turn out the way you want. Your only assignment is to live in faith and move forward into the unknown, knowing that there is no such place for the omniscient God who leads you forward. He has already gone ahead of you, preparing the way to ensure that you experience all that He has for you in every area of your life. Accept your life mission with enthusiasm.

Real Enthusiasm

Your life is hidden with Christ in God.
Colossians 3:3

The word *enthusiasm* is an interesting one. It comes from two Greek words, *en* (in) and *theos* (God). In years past, using the word *enthusiasm* was like using the words *blessed* or *godly*. It was recognized as a religious word.

The meaning of the word has been diluted and has now become associated with being excited, but for centuries people knew its real meaning. To be enthusiastic is to be united with Deity. You don't need to gain enthusiasm. You already have it, or to be more precise, you already have *Him*. You only need to act like who you are.

Is it hypocritical to act enthusiastic if you don't feel it? A hypocrite is a person who acts as if he is somebody that he really is not. Are you enthusiastic? Yes, because God lives in you. Then is it hypocritical to act like who you are even if you don't feel like it? Of course not. To the contrary, it is hypocritical behavior for you *not* to live with enthusiasm.

John Wesley once said, "When you set yourself on fire, people love to come and see you burn." Do you want to represent Christ well and make a supernatural impact? Then get on fire about life. Allow God's grace to ignite the fire of passion in you, and watch what happens!

All Things Sacred

*The earth is the LORD's, and all it contains,
The world, and those who dwell in it.*

PSALM 24:1

There is no area of your life that is segregated from your union to God. Because you are in Him, *everything is spiritual*. The Lord owns everything.

One of the greatest deceptions that has ever slipped into our minds is the idea that there is a difference between secular and sacred. There is no such dualism. Everything is sacred because of Christ's pervasive presence and He lives in you. The word *sacred* comes from the Latin word *sacer*, which denotes something uncommon because of its intimate association with the Divine.

You are one with God through Jesus Christ. Everything in your life is intimately associated with Him through your union with Him, thus making it sacred.

One man told me, "I like to keep my business life and my spiritual life separate from each other." What a sad thing. Do we leave Christ at home when we go to work? Does He go to our business appointments with us, but do we then politely instruct Him to sit quietly in the background? Our union with Christ defines the sum total of our lives.

Completely Equipped

His divine power has granted to us everything
pertaining to life and godliness, through
the true knowledge of Him who called
us by His own glory and excellence.

2 PETER 1:3

It is very important to believe that you aren't missing something in life that you need to develop. Your only need is to realize what you have already been given in Christ and apply those qualities in your life. You are able to live out of the resources you already possess in Christ. That, alone, is the secret to living the life you've been made to live.

Being who your Creator made you to be doesn't require you to *do* something. You need to *know* something—and that something is that your loving Father has already "given you the check." He has already "blessed (you) with every spiritual blessing in the heavenly places in Christ" (Ephesians 1:3). The only needed response is to cash the check! How is that done? Simply by believing that what God has said is true and *then* acting like you believe Him.

It is a matter of faith—believing what He tells us about Himself and about ourselves and then acting accordingly. You have all you need—both for time and eternity.

Excessive Burdens

We do not want you to be unaware, brethren, of our
affliction which came to us in Asia, that we were
burdened excessively, beyond our strength, so that we
despaired even of life; indeed, we had the sentence
of death within ourselves so that we would not
trust in ourselves, but in God who raises the dead.

2 Corinthians 1:8-9

A particular truth in this verse has been overlooked by most people today. Paul wrote that while he was in Asia he had a burden that was "beyond [his] strength." Other translations read that Paul said his problem was "far beyond our ability to endure"; "beyond our power"; "above our power."* It doesn't take a Greek Bible scholar to see what the Scripture clearly says in this text. The words are plain. Paul's burden was more than he could bear.

Why would God allow such a thing to happen? The Bible gives a clear answer. Second Corinthians 1:9 says it is "in order that we would not trust in ourselves, but in God who raises the dead." Your Father won't allow you to be tempted to sin beyond what you can resist, but He will allow troubles to become so heavy that you learn to trust Him and not yourself. Be assured that when you can't carry your burdens, He will.

*Respectively, New International Version, American Standard Version, and Young's Literal Translation.

A New World

You have not passed this way before.

JOSHUA 3:4

This may be one of the great understatements of the Bible. God's people were about to enter a new world—one that was so unlike anything they had ever known that they couldn't even imagine what it would be like. So it is with the person today who moves from the wilderness of religious legalism into the land of grace. To experience the reality of who we are in Christ is totally different from mere religious commitment. To compare living a religious lifestyle and experiencing a grace walk is to compare two different dimensions of living. They are more diametrically opposed than we can comprehend until we have crossed over from one to the other.

As you move further along in your own grace walk, remember that there is no place where legalistic religion and grace can intersect. Law and grace can never coexist together. You must move *out* of the wilderness of legalism *into* Canaan. To accept grace means to renounce legalism—a system of living in which you try to make spiritual progress or gain God's blessings based on what you do. It is a major move but one that will transform your life.

Spiritual Circumcision

In Him you were also circumcised with a circumcision made without hands, in the removal of the body of the flesh by the circumcision of Christ.

COLOSSIANS 2:11

God's covenant sign with His people under the Old Covenant of Law was circumcision. Why would He choose such a thing? It is because of what it depicts. He wanted the circumcision of Israel's men to be an object lesson pointing toward what would happen to His children under the new covenant of grace. Physical circumcision is the cutting away of a piece of skin on a man's body at the place from which life originates, and by which his gender (part of his identity) is identified. When the skin is cut away, it never grows back.

The apostle Paul points out that in this day of grace we have been circumcised "with a circumcision made without hands, in the removal of the body of the flesh by the circumcision of Christ." At the cross, God reached down and cut away from you the source of your old life. That source was the sin nature inherited from Adam. Through Jesus, God has removed it from you through your circumcision in Christ, and it will never grow back.

Healing in the Soul

*When they had finished circumcising all the nation,
they remained in their places in the camp until they
were healed. Then the LORD said to Joshua, "Today
I have rolled away the reproach of Egypt from you."*

JOSHUA 5:8-9

The whole time Israel wandered in the wilderness, her
men had not kept the covenant sign of circumcision.
Upon entering Canaan, they were circumcised in obedience to God. God had delivered them from their old
life in Egypt. Their circumcision verified that, but they
still needed to heal.

Your old life has been put to death. But don't
assume that everything connected with that lifestyle
will instantly disappear. Although your spirit is now
filled with the life of Jesus Christ, the soul must be gradually renewed, and that takes time. The soul is personality, consisting of your mind, will, and emotions. Part of
the ongoing sanctification process that the Holy Spirit
does in your life is to bring healing to your damaged
emotions and to renew your mind to the truth of God's
Word. The grace walk is not a lifestyle of sinless perfection, but it is a place where God can gradually bring
about the healing that we may need in our feelings and
beliefs.

Real Rest

The one who has entered His rest has himself also rested from his works, as God did from His.

HEBREWS 4:10

This verse is often used at funeral services to suggest that the one who has died "has now entered into God's rest and ceased from his own labors." The verse is often accompanied with words about heaven, suggesting that it is a place where we simply rest in Christ and enjoy Him forever.

That approach to the verse may sound good, but that isn't what it is actually teaching. Hebrews 4:11 says, "Let us be diligent to enter that rest, so that no one will fall, through following the same example of disobedience." If the previous verse refers to heaven, this verse must mean we need to be diligent to die.

No, the Bible isn't talking about physical death here. It is referring to the rest that is available when we give up our own struggles and enter into the rest of Jesus Christ. There are no more religious struggles when you know Christ as your resting place. Commit yourself into His hands right now and enjoy the inner rest that can come only from Him.

Manifold Grace

As each one has received a special gift,
employ it in serving one another as good
stewards of the manifold grace of God.

1 PETER 4:10

The apostle Peter used the word *manifold* to describe God's grace. The word means "multifaceted," like the fine cuts on a beautiful diamond. When one examines a flawless diamond under a bright light, its beauty is awesome. Then when the diamond is turned slightly so that the light is focused on a different facet, it may appear to be a totally different diamond, whose beauty equals or even surpasses what was previously seen. So it is with the grace of God. We will spend eternity marveling at His amazing grace as we continually examine it under the resplendent light and glory of the Son!

God's grace can be seen in your life in so many ways. It empowers you to do all that He has called you to do. It is grace that has caused you to become a holy person. Grace has brought you into union with your Triune God as a part of the eternal dance of love and life shared between the Father, Son, and Spirit.

There is no limit to the facets of beauty in grace. Praise God for it. Then share that grace with those you meet today.

Deserting Christ

I am amazed that you are so quickly deserting
Him who called you by the grace of Christ, for
a different gospel; which is really not another;
only there are some who are disturbing you,
and want to distort the gospel of Christ.

GALATIANS 1:6-7

Paul declares that the problem in the Galatian church was that the believers were deserting Jesus Christ. They were turning away from Him and focusing their attention on religious rules. They had understood perfectly the sole place of grace when they were saved, but now were being led to believe that their spiritual growth and maturity depended on themselves and what they did.

Paul makes clear that when we place our focus on religious rules, we are forsaking Jesus Christ. Our focus is to be on our relationship to Him, not rules. If you assess your life by how well you measure up to a list of responsibilities you imagine you have toward God, you will always feel an overshadowing sense of condemnation.

Nobody will ever live up to the picture of the person that the Law describes, because the Law is perfect and thus paints a picture of a perfect person, which we must be if we are to meet its demands. Thankfully, our perfection is found in Jesus Christ, not in perfect obedience to the Law.

Legally Dead

If you have died with Christ to the elementary principles of the world, why, as if you were living in the world, do you submit yourselves to decrees [religious rules], such as, "Do not handle, do not taste, do not touch!" (which all refer to things destined to perish with use)—in accordance with the commandments and teachings of men?

COLOSSIANS 2:20-22

Paul's question to the Colossians echoes down through the ages until today: "You have died to a system of religious rules, so why are you still acting like you have some connection to them?" The prevailing mindset of the modern church is that our lives are to be built around religious rules, but that is opposite from what the Bible teaches.

As long as a person lives in this world he is subject to the laws of the land. However, when he dies, the law no longer has any authority over him whatsoever. Even a murderer who dies is released from the law's demand on him.

You have died with Jesus Christ. It is now irrational to try to act as if religious laws have anything to do with you at all. You are free! Act like one who is free.

A Futile Attempt

When the woman saw that the tree was good
for food, and that it was a delight to the eyes,
and that the tree was desirable to make one
wise, she took from its fruit and ate; and she
gave also to her husband with her, and he ate.

Genesis 3:6

When Eve ate from the Tree of the Knowledge of Good and Evil, was she was trying to do something evil? If we think this, we miss a crucial point. Eve wasn't trying to do something wrong. She was trying to do something *good*. The serpent had told her that to eat from the tree would cause her to "be like God."

Eve's deception came in forgetting that she was *already* like God. She had been created in His image. It was an unnecessary and futile attempt to do anything to improve herself.

Don't fall for the lie that you need to do something to be more godly. Your union with Jesus Christ has created you in righteousness and holiness. Accept who you are, and don't sin by trying to do something God has said not to do, even if you think it's a good thing.

Loving Others

*A new commandment I give to you, that
you love one another, even as I have loved
you, that you also love one another.*

JOHN 13:34

Loving people. That's what it's all about in life. Whether it's the beggar on the street or a resident of an affluent neighborhood in suburbia, people want to know one thing—that they are loved. They are starving for it.

Sadly, the modern church often flounders in sharing the love of God with those around us for one simple reason: we don't fully understand how much we are loved by Him. Only when we understand that our lovableness isn't because of our performance but because of Christ in us will we feel the love of God for us. God doesn't love you in spite of you. He loves you because of Jesus and what He has done in you by making you a new creation. You aren't unlovable, because Christ, who is your Life, is completely lovable! Nobody is able to effectively express God's love to others until they have embraced His love for themselves. You must see yourself as a dear child of God who is dearly loved by Him. Having seen that, you become motivated to share it.

Glory to Glory

We all, with open face beholding as in a glass the
glory of the Lord, are changed into the same image
from glory to glory, even as by the Spirit of the Lord.

2 CORINTHIANS 3:18 KJV

Because of the finished work of Jesus Christ, you have received His nature. However, the work of the Holy Spirit is to cause you to mature in grace until your attitudes and actions completely conform to the righteousness of Christ that already fills your spirit. That change occurs through the ongoing work He does within you. It isn't something you accomplish.

Self-effort won't change any of us. If it worked, most of us would already have reached perfection because we have certainly tried…although we've failed. What does work in changing a person is the relentless grace of God operating in us as we focus on Him.

When we look at Jesus we see "the glory of the Lord," and in seeing Him we are "changed into the same image." It is a transformation that comes "from glory to glory"—from Him to us. Simply put, Jesus Christ is the mirror image of your true identity.

Cloud-Talk

The heavens declare the glory of God.
PSALM 19:1 NIV

Our Father can speak to us in so many ways that
are outside the box of religion. Clouds aren't religious.
The blue sky isn't religious. God doesn't communicate
only through church-talk, but also through cloud-talk.
These are only two of His many dialects.

The means by which God declares His love and
presence are without limit. Many ancient saints understood themselves to be living in a "God-bathed" world.
If you want to deeply experience intimacy with Him, it
helps immeasurably to view the world in the same way.
Our loving God reveals Himself in many ways. Jesus is
whispering to you right now, every day, in a thousand
ways, and many of them aren't religious. We need only
to be watching and aware.

Continual awareness of Christ in our daily lives
is inseparable from a hunger to know Him. Ask Him
to make Himself known to you, and then go through
your day with your eyes and ears open. As He leads you
into a growing awareness of His voice speaking in var-
ious ways, you will discover that heaven and earth are
His platform, a platform from which He constantly
declares His love for you.

Taste and See

O taste and see that the LORD is good!

PSALM 34:8

Once you have encountered your Lord's love up close and personal, you become addicted for life. It's impossible to experience enough of Him. It's as Jesus reveals Himself to us that we find ourselves hungering to know Him more intimately and to love Him more earnestly.

Speaking from his own experience, St. Augustine said, "You flashed, You shone; and You chased away my blindness. You became fragrant; and I inhaled and sighed for You. I tasted, and now hunger and thirst for You. You touched me; and I burned for Your embrace."

Spiritual hunger is the result of encountering Christ in our lives. That hunger then becomes the bridge by which we gain a heightened experience of Him with us in our circumstances. An authentic knowledge of Him will cause you to move through life with your spiritual antenna up, looking for signals of His presence nearby.

Ask the Lord to reach into your life like He did with Augustine. Then patiently wait for Him to flash, to shine, and to chase away your own blindness to His presence. He will come to you and do just that.

Finding Quietness

*I urge that entreaties and prayers, petitions
and thanksgivings, be made on behalf
of all men, for kings and all who are in
authority, so that we may lead a tranquil
and quiet life in all godliness and dignity.*

1 TIMOTHY 2:1-2

The Bible teaches that our goal should be to "lead a tranquil and quiet life in all godliness and dignity." In fact, we're instructed to seek earnestly to "lead a quiet life" (1 Thessalonians 4:11). These days, quietness and rest from activity are almost obsolete in the culture, yet the Bible stresses the importance of intentionally setting aside a time and quiet place in our lifestyles.

Ancient Christians lived in a culture that was more conducive to quiet reflection. There weren't so many competing demands for their time and attention as we have. Today it is important to choose to stand against the current of our culture by designating time for contemplative reflection and prayer.

Do you sense an inner stirring to withdraw from the busy demands of life and meet Jesus Christ in a quiet place? If so, you can be assured that you're hearing the gentle voice of Jesus inviting you to come away with Him for a while. Accept His invitation to meet Him in a quiet place, and the reward will be great.

Godly Contentment

Godliness actually is a means of great gain
when accompanied by contentment.

1 Timothy 6:6

A contented heart is a heart at peace. It's the main ingredient in the lives of those who live with an underlying sense of well-being. Contentment is an inner stillness caused by knowing our lives are firmly on the course God has set for us. Contentment is the opposite of restlessness.

Contentment means being set free from an all-consuming goal to achieve and attain more and more. Real contentment comes when we begin to focus on spiritual depth instead of the superficial breadth lauded by modern standards.

Your life is hidden with God in Christ. Your roots are in heaven even as you read this. Your contentment comes from that life, not this one. Don't look for contentment in this world.

In modern culture, many voices call out for your devotion. Choose which voice you will listen and respond to. If you are to experience contentment in your grace walk, you must disassociate yourself from the voices that would interfere with intimacy with Jesus. Not because they are inherently wrong, but because there are too many. A wise person simply can't be focused on everything that calls out for his or her attention. Be wise.

Sovereign Supervision

The LORD has established His throne in the heavens,
And His sovereignty rules over all.

PSALM 103:19

The events of your life aren't unfolding by random chance. A sovereign God rules over what happens in this small space-time box called Earth. The world is not hanging in the balance, with the outcome yet to be determined. Some people seem to believe that the throngs of heaven are on one side of the stadium and the demons of hell are on the other, each hoping their side wins. Within the context of this twisted theology, it becomes man's decisions that determine who wins—and meanwhile, God is keeping His fingers crossed. With that perspective, it's no wonder that so few find spiritual rest!

That line of thinking is nothing less than religious humanism. It is an insult to God's sovereignty. It puts man in the driver's seat and makes God nothing more than a nervous passenger who is doing all He can do to make sure everything turns out all right. God is portrayed as sometimes encouraging us, sometimes threatening us, but always hoping that we will respond in the right way.

All of heaven isn't holding its breath waiting to see how things turn out in the end. Your God superintends this world and your life. Affirm His sovereignty and experience peace as the result.

The Inner Man

*…that He would grant you, according to the
riches of His glory, to be strengthened with
power through His Spirit in the inner man.*

EPHESIANS 3:16

Real strength is found in what Paul called "the inner man." He understood that life is to be lived from within the inner man. To be strengthened through God's Spirit in the inner man is to experience the ministry of the Spirit of Christ within us, living each moment in recognition that He alone is our source of life.

It's from the inside that the indwelling Christ will transform you. It's so easy to get it backward. Legalistic religion seeks to reform us from the outside, stressing that if we will simply behave in certain ways we will be changed. The effect of legalism is always the same. Jesus said people might clean up well on the outside, but on the inside, still be full of filth.

Refuse to fall into the self-help perversion of grace that would tell you that you need to improve what you do outwardly to facilitate inward change. The indwelling Christ is capable of changing you from the inside out. Protect and nurture your inner life, and outward actions will fall into line.

The Witness of Scripture

*You search the Scriptures because you think
that in them you have eternal life; it is these
that testify about Me; and you are unwilling
to come to Me so that you may have life.*

JOHN 5:39-40

The mistake many people make when they approach the Bible is that they see it as an end unto itself. They don't realize that the Bible isn't a destination but a road sign that points to the True Destination. That destination is Jesus Christ.

The Pharisees studied the Scriptures as much as anybody could, but Jesus indicated that they had entirely missed the point. He plainly said that life isn't found in the Scriptures but in Him.

As you read your Bible, it is important to understand that your primary focus isn't to find principles for living. It isn't to gain knowledge of Scripture for the sake of knowing more. The main purpose for time spent in the Bible is to encounter Jesus!

Think of the Bible as a photo album. In the New Testament, Jesus is clearly seen standing in the front of the picture on every page. In the Old Testament, He stands in the background of the photograph. Come to the Bible expecting a revelation of Jesus Christ and you won't be disappointed.

Fellowship Together

*If we walk in the Light as He Himself is in the
Light, we have fellowship with one another.*

1 John 1:7

Because you are in the light of God's grace, you have
the joy of celebrating divine life with others. The biblical word *fellowship* denotes intimate participation with
each other.

This kind of community was a foundational aspect
of the growth of the early church. The second chapter
of Acts portrays a group of people who laughed and
loved, who shared meals and money; people who took
seriously the practice of partying under the direction
of God's Spirit. They would have fully affirmed C.S.
Lewis's claim that "joy is the serious business of heaven."

A spirit of carefree, lighthearted, God-centered cel-
ebration is often conspicuously absent in the lives of
many in the modern church. When did we begin to
take ourselves so seriously? What urgent matters have
we allowed to rob us of our playful spirit? We are going
to live forever. How important can things really be that
won't even be remembered a hundred years from now?
There's no doubt about it, most of us need to lighten up.

Would you like to enjoy life more? Find others who
love Jesus too and have fun together. It's the sort of thing
that delights your heavenly Father when He sees it.

Mighty Works

*For this purpose also I labor, striving according
to His power, which mightily works within me.*

COLOSSIANS 1:29

Experiencing the grace walk is to know the invigorating reality of Jesus Christ literally expressing Himself through you with your personality, your thoughts, and your unique characteristics. It is a life energized by divinity—as opposed to a religious struggle that originates from your own frail humanity.

Grace doesn't cause a person to become lazy or uninterested in spiritual service. To the contrary, the grace of Jesus motivates us to serve with the power of heaven pulsing through our actions. Paul used the word *labor* to describe his actions. The word denotes the idea of work on steroids!

Those who suggest that grace leads to passivity haven't personally experienced the joy of seeing mighty works that make an eternal difference flowing from their lives without a struggle. Your lifestyle in serving God isn't passive, but it is effortless because it isn't by your determination that you work. It is by His power that mightily works in you.

Yield yourself to the Spirit of Christ. Ask Him to work mightily through you in your daily routine. He will accomplish the miraculous through you, His chosen vessel.

Guaranteed Provision

*Make sure that your character is free from the
love of money, being content with what you
have; for He Himself has said, "I will never
desert you, nor will I ever forsake you."*

HEBREWS 13:5

Every day we are bombarded with advertising that
tries to convince us we don't have everything to fulfill us until we purchase that product. Advertising is
designed to create a sense of need in those it reaches.
Grace empowers you to live above that enticement.

Money isn't evil, but the love of money will cause a
person to think and act in sad ways. Guard your character in this area. Know that Jesus Christ is yours and
that your source for everything you could ever need is
found in Him. Don't look to the faucet from which the
water flows as your source. Realize that there is a River
of Life that flows through the temporal faucet from
which you drink.

There will never be a time when you are stranded
without provision, because He has promised to never
leave or forsake you. Think of the times He has met
your needs in the past. He will not fail you now or ever.
Trust Him and grow in the certainty that He is more
than enough.

The New Creation

*Put on the new self, which in the likeness of God has
been created in righteousness and holiness of the truth.*

EPHESIANS 4:24

You are a new creation in Jesus Christ. Any religious
self-improvement program is a denial of the new creation He has made. There is no need to improve yourself. The only need is to understand the truth about
who you already are. You have been created in righteousness and holiness. Those two words define who
you are at the core.

Paul didn't tell the Ephesians to become righteous
and holy because he knew they already were. He told
them to "put on the new self." The imagery is one of
wearing the garment you have been given. Put on holiness and righteousness in your daily lifestyle because
that is who you are.

Dead religion tries to impose a works-oriented system on its adherents. Such a system will put them in
lasting bondage by causing them to seek to accomplish
something for themselves that God has already accomplished for them. Don't fall prey to that system. Con-
fess your righteousness in Christ and affirm that you are
holy. To do that is to give glory to Him by agreeing in
faith with what He has said and done.

Proper Boasting

*In Christ Jesus I have found reason for boasting
in things pertaining to God. For I will not
presume to speak of anything except what Christ
has accomplished through me, resulting in the
obedience of the Gentiles by word and deed.*

<small>ROMANS 15:17-18</small>

Legalistic religion fuels pride by causing us to think that the spiritual progress we believe we have made is the result of our own dedication. Grace strips away human pride by causing us to know that any authentic spiritual growth we experience is the result of God's goodness and nothing else. The two viewpoints stand in diametric opposition to one another.

Paul might have boasted about his credentials, his accomplishments, and the sacrifices he had made in spreading the gospel. However, as one to whom God had clearly revealed His grace, Paul knew better. The only boasting he did was to brag about the goodness of Christ. While he delighted in the way the Gentiles had received the gospel message under his preaching, he acknowledged that all the glory belonged to Christ.

Beware of thinking that your skill sets are what bring you success in life. Any endeavor in which you succeed is the direct result of Jesus Christ working through you. Give Him the glory and it will only get better.

Favor and Union

*I pastured the flock doomed to slaughter, hence
the afflicted of the flock. And I took for myself
two staffs: the one I called Favor and the other
I called Union; so I pastured the flock.*

ZECHARIAH 11:7

This obscure verse hidden away among the Minor
Prophets gives a powerful prescription for godly leadership. Zechariah described taking a flock from the
greedy shepherds who had controlled them. The first
thing he did was to select two shepherd staffs. One he
called "Favor," and the other he called "Union."

What tools for leadership in the hands of every
godly leader! *Favor* is the disposition of kindness
toward those you lead. It is closely related to grace in
that it is an expression of loving concern for those in
your charge.

Union refers to a binding together between the
shepherd and those he leads. A godly leader doesn't
stand aloof and disconnected. His life is intertwined
with those he leads because he genuinely cares about
them. He doesn't say, "Go do this," but "Let's go do
this!"

Apply these principles in your leadership of those
under your charge and you will be behaving like another
Great Shepherd. Favor and Union are His staffs too.

True Justice

Thus has the LORD of hosts said, "Dispense
true justice and practice kindness and
compassion each to his brother."

ZECHARIAH 7:9

Grace is the mother of justice. Divine justice is different from the polluted concept of human justice. Revenge isn't justice. On the other hand, restoration is a perfect expression of justice.

Allow the Scripture and the Spirit to renew your mind about the meaning of justice. Seek to facilitate divine justice in every arena where you have personal influence. Look at others and ask yourself how Jesus Christ would treat that person and then strive toward seeing that they receive that kind of treatment.

Justice transcends political parties, religious sects, and philosophical positions. To dispense justice by practicing kindness and compassion toward others is to express the heart of our Father. To dispense the justice of the Father is to walk in sync with the Spirit and the Word.

If dispensing justice hasn't been a priority in your life, ask the Holy Spirit to show you occasions and means by which you can bring this expression of divine love into your grace walk. Life isn't fair, but God is gracious. Show that to others by your actions and influence.

Dying to Live

Whoever wishes to save his life will lose it; but
whoever loses his life for My sake will find it.

MATTHEW 16:25

The dynamics of your grace walk are very different from the attempt to live independently. Most people think that achieving the quality of life they want requires several types of effort: building up what they can in any way they can, preserving their assets, and pushing toward increase. That's not how things work in the kingdom of God.

Jesus said that if you want to save your life, you will lose it—but if you lose your life for His sake you will find it. That sounds backward to human reason, but that's the way it really is. We gain by giving up.

This principle of self-sacrifice is the natural order in the world of grace. We die to live. We become weak to experience strength. We are brought down to be raised up. We give away and then have more. Do you see how God's way of grace works?

The key is to abandon all ideas of self-preservation and cast yourself completely into the hands of the One who alone has the ability to determine your future. Lay down your life for His glory and begin to really live.

Abandoning Anxiety

…casting all your anxiety on Him,
because He cares for you.

1 PETER 5:7

The essence of anxiety is a sense of unease about a particular outcome. It comes from imagining the future without your Father's involvement in it. It is projecting a faithless imagination into the days ahead and seeing the worst possible outcome.

When we understand the meaning of the grace walk, living in such a way is completely unnecessary. The One who lives in you has promised that His yoke is *easy*—one of ease. He has united you together with Him in His yoke. He has taken the lead in guiding you where you are headed and in providing the power by which you will get there.

Don't imagine a godless future in your circumstance. It's easy to say we believe in Him—but it is at moments when we are tested that faith becomes paramount to our peace of mind. Exercise your faith now.

Jesus is Lord over your past, present, and future. His nature will be the same tomorrow as it has always been. God is love, and that will never change. He cares for you—deeply cares for you, so cast your anxiety on Him and leave it there.

Abandonment Is Impossible

Can a woman forget her nursing child
And have no compassion on the son of her womb?
Even these may forget, but I will not forget you.

When a mother abandons her newborn baby, the the event usually makes the news. People shake their heads in disbelief because there is no bond quite like that between a new mother and her nursing child. It is a mother's nature to love and nurture her child.

There is almost no limit to the sacrifices that a mother would make for her baby. She would do almost anything for the well-being of that child. Nothing is too much, it seems.

God wants you to know that the likelihood of a mother forsaking and forgetting her child may be small, but the chance of Him forgetting you is nonexistent. His love for you will cause Him to pour out compassion on you forever. No circumstance, no sin, no problem—nothing at all could ever affect His disposition and actions toward you.

You are His precious child. He gave His Son's life for you so that He could give His life to you. His love for you never vacillates for any reason. You can take comfort in knowing that you are His and will forever be the focus of His love.

Miraculous Peace

He Himself is our peace…
EPHESIANS 2:14

To ask Jesus to give you peace is redundant. Peace isn't something He gives you to sustain you during troubled times. He *is* peace—and to experience His indwelling life is to experience peace that passes understanding. Because Christ is the source of your life, there is never a time when peace cannot be your default setting.

In John 14:27, Jesus told his disciples, "Peace I leave with you; My peace I give to you; not as the world gives do I give to you. Do not let your heart be troubled, nor let it be fearful." The world offers peace based on the hope that things will turn out okay. Jesus gives a different kind of peace. He has given you Himself. He will be your source of peace regardless of how things turn out in your situation.

You can trust Him with the circumstances that are emotionally and mentally challenging. Your peace isn't in a specific outcome but in the one who assures you that there is no need to be troubled or fearful. Whatever comes, it will be all right because He is with you to carry you through it.

Wise Choices

The LORD gives wisdom;
From His mouth come knowledge and understanding.

PROVERBS 2:6

Wisdom is more than knowledge. It is knowing what to do with knowledge. The Old Testament promised those who sought the Lord that He would give them wisdom. What an encouragement that must have been to them.

However, the grace walk is even better. You live under a New Covenant, in which your Father doesn't offer to give you wisdom. Instead, He already *has* given it to you in Jesus Christ. The apostle Paul wrote, "By His doing you are in Christ Jesus, who became to us wisdom from God" (1 Corinthians 1:30).

You possess divine wisdom because you have Wisdom living in you! Don't lean on your own understanding. When you face a decision, pray and ask Him to express wisdom in your thoughts.

Then confidently make your decision knowing that you didn't do it alone. Don't second-guess the decision you've made. Move forward in faith that, just as He expressed wisdom in you as you made the decision, He will guide you to execute the choice you have made. To live this way is to walk in faith.

Honoring Others

Be devoted to one another in brotherly love;
give preference to one another in honor.

ROMANS 12:10

Most people see this world as dog-eat-dog. That cynical view has nurtured a cultural mindset that suggests that you had better look out for yourself because nobody else is going to do it for you. Many might be accused of getting to where they are by climbing on the backs of those they have exploited. It often seems that selfishness rules the day.

As one who practices the grace walk, you have a wonderful opportunity to declare Jesus to other people simply by the way you treat them. Because of underlying feelings of insecurity, many people are hungry to be affirmed. Their hunger is your opportunity to show unconditional love.

"Give preference to one another in honor," the Bible says. One translation says, "Take delight in honoring each other."* Gracious words and deeds toward others are potent with divine life.

Who can you honor today? Affirm the inherent value of another person and you will discover that your words can transform a life. The One who raised a dead man from a tomb by speaking to Him also will speak to others through you. Speak love and life to those around you.

*New Living Translation

Guarding Our Words

*A fool uttereth all his mind: but a wise
man keepeth it in till afterwards.*

PROVERBS 29:11 KJV

So many conflicts could be avoided if people simply understood the truth of this verse. The Bible says that it is a fool who speaks whatever he is thinking at the moment. A wise person guards his words and speaks at the right time.

Have you heard someone say, "Well, I just say whatever I think!" That person has unwittingly revealed something negative about himself. In contrast, a wise person knows when to speak up and when to be quiet.

As you deal with people, some of them will irritate you. Sometimes people or situations can be so annoying that we find words rising up in our minds that almost demand to be spoken. Don't give in to that impulse.

You are empowered by grace and have authority over what you say and don't say. Don't give life to angry thoughts by inappropriately expressing them. There is a proper time, place, and manner for expressing thoughts in words. Be sure that when you speak, it is a godly response and not an impulsive reaction.

Changing the Environment

A joyful heart makes a cheerful face.
PROVERBS 15:13

As a grace walker, you have a great potential within you that people seldom exercise. You have the ability to affect every environment in which you function. Your very presence in a room can change the atmosphere.

Have you known people who seem to brighten up a room simply by their presence? You may have known others who had the opposite effect. Still others respond to whatever the prevailing mood may be.

The grace of God in you can enable you to be a sort of "thermostat" in every place you find yourself. While others may act like thermometers and adjust to the atmosphere around them, you have the ability to change it. Jesus Christ lives inside you, and He is your source of joy.

Walk in faith and allow the joy of Christ that lives inside you to affect your whole demeanor. Smile. Laugh. Love others. Be a change agent wherever you are. As a conduit of grace you can have a greater influence than you might have imagined.

Don't follow the crowd. Choose to let your outward demeanor be an expression of your inner condition, where Jesus Christ lives.

Disarming Negative Thoughts

*...we are taking every thought captive
to the obedience of Christ.*

2 CORINTHIANS 10:5

Contrary to how it may sometimes seem, you have control over your thoughts. Those who don't understand this will be held captive by thoughts constantly flooding their minds and needlessly exciting negative emotions. The battleground is indeed in the mind. For that reason, it is important to understand the Spirit-led strategy for handling counterproductive thoughts that bombard our minds.

The strategy begins by recognizing that not every thought you have originated from you. Make no mistake—the enemy can introduce a thought into your mind. If you don't know better, he will then try to cause you to believe that it is your own thought so you'll either act on it or else condemn yourself for having it.

Don't fall for that ploy. When a thought comes to your mind that isn't in line with the nature of Christ (which is now also your nature), renounce and reject it. Then for good measure, affirm the truth of the matter as you expose the wrong thought to the light of your faith in Christ. Don't let lies find a home in your mind. Reject them immediately and stand strong in the Truth.

Loving Solidarity

Rejoice with those who rejoice, and
weep with those who weep.

ROMANS 12:15

One of the opportunities to share authentic love with somebody is to identify with them in the heights and depths of life. Empathy for another person's joy or grief is most often a sure way to strengthen your relationship with them.

When a person celebrates, your expression of joy enhances the experience by multiplying the joy. When somebody hurts, your sincere sympathy is a healing balm. Both the bliss and burdens of life are best experienced with others.

When people are hurting, don't think that you need to offer an answer. Just be there to express your loving concern. Biblical promises, albeit true, can sometimes be perceived as canned responses if spoken at an inappropriate time. Attempted explanations or inspirational platitudes have nowhere near the healing power of a loving touch or gentle word of shared sorrow.

It isn't your job to fix people, but it is your privilege to stand with them in the intense moments of life. Loving solidarity has miraculous power that leaves its mark on a person's life forever. It is actions like this that show the heart of the One who loves people most.

Seeing Miracles

Men of Israel, listen to these words: Jesus the
Nazarene [was] a man attested to you by God
with miracles and wonders and signs which
God performed through Him in your midst...

ACTS 2:22

The Bible says that it was God who performed the miracles, wonders, and signs through Jesus. Our Lord did not live out of his own ability. He lived out of the infinite ability of His Father. Peter stresses the fact that Jesus was a man who relied on His Father to accomplish His work. If Jesus chose to depend totally on His Father to animate and empower His lifestyle, how foolish it is to think we can do anything for God by our own natural abilities!

A miracle is an act of God that defies natural explanation. Do you know when miracles happen? A person will see the miraculous work of God in and through him to the extent that he renounces self-sufficiency and rests in the all-sufficient Holy Spirit within him.

If you want your grace walk to be marked by the kind of miraculous power Jesus knew in this world, don't depend on yourself. Instead, trust Him to do His works through you in the normal flow of your lifestyle. As He does, it will be apparent to you and others that it is Him at work, and He will get the credit for it.

Personal Righteousness

…even the righteousness of God which is by faith of Jesus Christ unto all and upon all them that believe.

ROMANS 3:22 KJV

Many people simply don't understand the reality of the righteousness that is ours in Jesus Christ. Because they don't *feel* righteous, they interpret what the Bible says about the matter in a way that falls short of the truth. To experience the grace walk, it is vital to recognize that God took away your unrighteousness and gave you His righteousness. You have been given the righteous nature of Jesus.

Those who fail to understand this gift are doomed to a legalistic lifestyle, always trying to achieve righteousness by their works. Grace is the means by which God gives us righteousness. It is not something we achieve, but rather something that we receive in Christ. The Bible plainly calls it a "gift" in Romans 5:17.

Don't fall short in your understanding by thinking you aren't literally righteous. Some would say that God only *sees* us that way. They would argue that our position is one of righteousness, but our condition is that we are unrighteous. Exactly what could this mean? Are they suggesting that God sees something that isn't really there?

You *are* righteous. It's not a complicated issue. Accept His righteousness as your own. If the grace walk is anything, it is a righteous identity.

The Law's Purpose

The Law came in so that the
transgression would increase…
Romans 5:20

There is much confusion today about the purpose for God's Law. Some think He gave the Law to subdue sin in the world. Have you believed that God gave the Law so that people would keep it and sin would be subdued? That is not its purpose.

The Bible clearly teaches that the purpose of the Law is to reveal sin. It doesn't generate sin, but it does most definitely stimulate it within any person who embraces it. It brings it from beneath the surface right out into the open. Today's verse says that the Law *increases*, not decreases, sinning.

First Corinthians 15:56 tells us, "The power of sin is the law." Rules don't keep a person from sinning. They cause them to sin! So the unwitting Christian who determines to build their life around spiritual rules is setting themselves up for a lifestyle filled with failure!

The Law was given to Israel in response to her self-righteousness, so that she would see her sin and turn to God. That Law was never given to you. Jesus, however, has been given to you. So trust Him and give up any misguided notions you may have about needing to keep religious rules of any kind.

Your Daily Walk

As you have received Christ Jesus
the Lord, so walk in Him.

COLOSSIANS 2:6

The Bible teaches that we are to walk as Christians in the same way we came to know God in the beginning—through appropriating His grace by faith. Grace started our walk and will sustain it. The responsibility is all on our Father to teach us to walk. Our only role is to trust Him.

A legalistic approach to the Christian life is built on the foundation of fear. It is the fear that we won't actually live a godly life apart from the coercive or persuasive pressure normally associated with rules. Yet genuine grace will motivate a person to live a godly lifestyle more than a thousand laws could ever do.

A legalist greatly underestimates the power of the indwelling Holy Spirit. When we know that we are free from the law, we will discover that God's indwelling Spirit will motivate us to serve based on our relationship to Jesus, not because of external demands to perform.

Relax and enjoy your grace walk. You don't have to manufacture anything spiritual to please God. He is already pleased with you. So rest in His acceptance and live each day in calm faith.

Obedience in Grace

If you love Me, you will keep My commandments.
JOHN 14:15

Does the fact that we aren't bound to religious rules mean that we ignore New Testament commands? Didn't Jesus say that if we love him, we will keep His commandments? He did indeed. Yet when grace rules a person's life, he or she will approach the commandments of the New Testament with a totally different attitude than the legalist.

Legalism presents the commandments as divine ultimatums coming from a harsh Judge. When law rules a person, the inflection of Jesus' words is heard like this: "If you love me, you *had better* keep my commandments." A grace walk causes us to face the commandments with eager anticipation, not with fear and a feeling of intimidation. We properly understand the words of Jesus when he said, "If you love me, you *will* keep my commandments."

John stressed the relationship between love and our obedience to God's commandments when he said, "This is the love of God, that we keep His commandments; and His commandments are not burdensome" (1 John 5:3). When we are walking in grace it is no burden to obey the commandments of God. It is a pleasure to be obedient!

Freedom over Sins

*Those who are according to the flesh set their
minds on the things of the flesh, but those who
are according to the Spirit, the things of the
Spirit. For the mind set on the flesh is death, but
the mind set on the Spirit is life and peace.*

ROMANS 8:5-6

What you think about is important. In fact, in this
text Paul asserts that whatever you set your mind upon
will ultimately determine your behavior. If we set our
mind on the sins of the flesh, it should come as no
surprise when our behavior matches our mindset. We
guarantee our own failure when we decide to overcome
sin by concentrating on it.

It will make no difference that we ask God to help
us. God won't bless our efforts to deliver ourselves from
sin. He wants to use our futile efforts to achieve victory
over sin to force our attention toward Jesus. As long as
we try to gain victory through our behavior, He will
patiently wait until we have exhausted all our efforts.
Then He will do for us what we can't do for ourselves. It
is at that point that we are ready to receive His answer.

Is there something you want to overcome? Stop
focusing on it and set your mind on Christ. He will
cause you to experience the freedom you want.

The Downward Pull

*Wretched man that I am! Who will set
me free from the body of this death?*

ROMANS 7:24

Overcoming sins in your life involves asking the right question. Paul presented the definitive question regarding sin when he asked, "Who will set me free from the body of this death?" He recognized that the key to victory doesn't come by asking "what" or "how." The key to victory over sin is a Who.

Asking what or how suggests that there must be a plan or method that will enable us to overcome sin. God's provision for our sins is not a plan, but the Person of Jesus Christ.

As you depend upon Christ, trusting Him to be your life source at every moment, you will experience victory over sin. However, at any moment that you might decide to function apart from relying on Christ, sin will always be the bitter fruit.

There is no other possibility. There is no middle ground. Either you are choosing to depend entirely on Christ or you aren't. When your lifestyle is absorbed by your intimacy with Him, victory is the natural expression of His life. You will soar above the downward pull of indwelling sin because you are carried along by the gentle breeze of His love.

Grace, Not Law

*Sin shall not be master over you, for you
are not under law but under grace.*

ROMANS 6:14

Grace is a system of living whereby God blesses us because we are in Jesus Christ, and for no other reason at all. Yet many people are miserable because they still live with an Old Testament viewpoint—a viewpoint that causes them to try to stay in God's favor by good behavior.

The Law demands, "Your behavior must improve to receive God's blessings!" It is simply wrong to believe we make spiritual progress or gain God's blessings based on what we do. It is opposite of the grace walk.

Grace is the voice of God saying, "I will bless you until your behavior does improve!" When grace fills us, we want to live a consistently godly lifestyle. It is the faithfulness of God that causes our heart to be changed so we are motivated to godly living by desire, not a sense of religious duty.

Don't struggle against sins you may see in your life. Instead, meditate on the reality that your Father loves you no matter how you behave. His love really is unconditional. As you immerse yourself in His love you will find that your desires are changed so that sin loses its magnetic attraction.

Praise to Our Creator

*Worthy are You, our Lord and our God, to
receive glory and honor and power; for You
created all things, and because of Your
will they existed, and were created.*

REVELATION 4:11

What a song from heaven! God willed the physical universe to exist, and so it did. Why did God create the universe? Proverbs 16:4 tells us that "the LORD has made everything for its own purpose." He did it for one simple reason—because it was what He wanted. The psalmist said, "He spoke, and it was done; He commanded, and it stood fast" (Psalm 33:9).

The universe exists because it was the will of God. The stars don't hang up there on nothing. They are held in place by the will of an omnipotent God. The tide at the beach doesn't just coincidentally stop at its boundaries and return to the sea. It is ordered back by divine design. The earth isn't spinning on its axis because of its own momentum. That's the will of God at work. He designed it that way. The inanimate world in which we live conforms to the will of God.

If that is true of the inanimate world, imagine how much more it must be true of you! Your God created you because He *wanted* you. You were the desire of His heart before your mother ever got one glimpse of you. You have been eternally wanted.

Ruthless People

This Man, delivered over by the predetermined plan and foreknowledge of God, you nailed to the cross by the hands of godless men and put Him to death. But God raised Him up again.

ACTS 2:23-24

Has anybody ever been terribly unfair to you? Have you ever been almost destroyed by the ruthlessness of another? You're not alone.

The greatest offense ever committed against a man was what was done to Jesus by those who opposed Him. They tortured and killed the perfect Son of God. The amazing thing about the mistreatment of Jesus (and you) is the Father's ability to redeem it.

God is bigger than the wrong men do. Human beings were completely responsible for crucifying the Son of God. "You nailed [Him] to the cross," Peter said. But God was sovereign over even this, and in fact, had planned it before the foundation of the world: Christ was "delivered over by the predetermined plan and foreknowledge of God." Do you see how the two fit together? We do have an awesome God!

Mentally release those who have treated you with unfairness or even cruelty. Don't live in the past. Your God stands above all that has happened in your life. He can redeem and use those things for your good and His glory.

Unwavering Trust

With respect to the promise of God, he did not waver in unbelief but grew strong in faith, giving glory to God, and being fully assured that what God had promised, He was able also to perform.

ROMANS 4:20-21

Although he lived long ago, Abraham had the same kind of challenges and trials we have as we go through life. He had to decide how to respond when what he saw didn't match what God had said.

God had promised Abraham a son in his old age—when it was humanly impossible. We may be tempted to say to the apostle Paul, "That's an interesting statement, Paul. Are we talking about the same man? I'm thinking of the one who had to have God tell him again and again that He was going to follow through with what He had said. The man who had relations with a servant girl because he was convinced his biological clock was quickly winding down. That's the guy you're saying didn't waver in unbelief?"

"That's the one," Paul would answer. Faith doesn't mean we have to feel strong and confident at every moment. It means we just keep clinging to God, even through our highs and lows.

When you're tempted to think you have wobbly faith, take another look at Abraham. Then look at your faithful God and praise Him for His goodness.

The Divine Perspective

We have the mind of Christ.

1 Corinthians 2:16

As God's child, you have divine ability to see life through the eyes of faith, allowing Christ to see and live and work and love through you. You are a conduit of His life into this world. The One who controls it all lives in and through you. Let that be a truth that stirs your faith.

Don't worry about stumbling as you move ahead in your grace walk. Go ahead and act in faith. Live courageously, believing that He wants you to grow through every experience.

The apostle Paul once said, "When I was child, I used to speak like a child, think like a child, reason like a child; when I became a man, I did away with childish things" (1 Corinthians 13:11). There's nothing wrong with being a child, but to remain a child is abnormal. The time has come to act in maturity in regard to discovering and doing what you sense God has planned for you. If you'll step out in faith, you'll see that He will faithfully guide you and make sure you reach the destination He has in mind for you.

Saints by Calling

To the church of God which is at Corinth,
to those who have been sanctified in
Christ Jesus, saints by calling…

1 CORINTHIANS 1:2

Paul wrote to the church in Corinth and identified them as "saints by calling." To be "sanctified," or to become a "saint," means that God has set you apart as special. He sees you as His beloved possession for His exclusive use.

Notice that Paul calls the believers in the Corinthian church "saints," even though he wrote two of his longest letters trying to correct problems in their attitudes and behavior. "Saint" is a description of their identity, not their actions, and the same is true of you. Knowing who you are changes everything! You are then equipped to act out of your true identity instead of your feelings. Feelings can deceive you. But when you realize you have been set apart for a divine purpose, you can gradually bring negative feelings into alignment with the truth of God's Word—the truth that you are special and blessed.

Refuse to see yourself as less than a saint in Jesus Christ. Not just so you will have a positive self-image, but because it's important for you to have a *biblical* self-image. You are who God says you are. How you feel or behave doesn't change that.

Walking in Light

You were formerly darkness, but now you are
Light in the Lord; walk as children of Light.

EPHESIANS 5:8

The order of thought in this verse is critically important to recognize. Notice what it does not say: "If you children of darkness start acting like children of Light, you can become Light." It begins with what God has done. He has already changed our identities from darkness to Light in Christ; now He calls us to recognize it and be who He made us to be.

The truth is that you are in the Light. You are in the Light at every moment because, through Jesus Christ, you are continuously in God. "God is light and in Him is no darkness at all," the apostle John wrote.

Since God is Light and can never contain darkness and you are in God, you can never be in darkness. We may not always be able to see the light in a situation; we may even willfully blindfold ourselves by sinning, but that doesn't change the fact that we're in the Light. A man wearing a blindfold over his eyes may not see light even when he is standing under a bright floodlight, but that doesn't change the reality that he is still in the light.

You are a child of the Light. Believe it. Then walk in the light of His life with confidence that there is no darkness in you because you are in Him.

Acknowledging Him

In all your ways acknowledge Him,
And He will make your paths straight.

Proverbs 3:6

Acknowledging God is a mindset. It is an attitude toward the Lord of complete trust. It is not some kind of constant verbal reassurance to Him that we are acknowledging Him. It doesn't mean we're going through our day saying, "Lord, I'm acknowledging you, I'm acknowledging you, I'm acknowledging you…" It doesn't even necessarily require that we express it verbally at all. Nor does it necessarily even mean consciously, as if every moment we are aware we are acknowledging Him, thinking to ourselves, "I'm trusting, I'm trusting, I'm trusting…" It's not praying a certain number of prayers to reassure Him or ourselves that we are acknowledging Him.

To acknowledge our Father is to trust Him completely. It means calmly resting in the sufficiency of Jesus Christ within us. It is an underlying perspective, not a religious mantra we chant in our minds.

The One who loves you more than any other lays out your course for you. He delights in revealing his purposes to you. Know that He is your life, and trust totally in Him that He will direct your path.

Follow Me

As He passed by, He saw Levi the son of Alphaeus
sitting in the tax booth, and He said to him,
"Follow Me!" And he got up and followed Him.

MARK 2:14

There have been many religious founders, teachers, gurus, and philosophers in the history of the world. All of them have taught moral laws, words of wisdom, doctrines—they have said, in effect, "Go this way." In contrast, Jesus Christ is unique. The center of His teaching was not "Keep these rules," "go this way," or "follow these practices." Jesus always pointed to Himself and simply said, "Follow me."

You have been created as a unique follower of Christ. The beauty of our God is so immense and awesome that He has shared Himself with us all. His purpose is to reveal Himself in this world through his body, the church. Each of us has an opportunity to show His life in a way that is unique to us. You have the ability to demonstrate the Christ-Life in a way that is different from anybody who has ever lived or ever will live, because there will never be another you!

To follow Jesus is to walk in sync with His Spirit. As you do, you will display His life and others will be drawn to Him. Follow Him. It's a simple command with eternal implications.

Fearless Living

*God has not given us a spirit of timidity, but
of power and love and discipline.*

2 Timothy 1:7

"Timidity" translates a word that can also be translated "cowardice." It means cringing, paralyzing fear. This kind of fear comes from our imaginations, especially imaginary scenarios of the future. It's fear that has no basis in truth. It grows out of unbelief and is destructive. Notice that Paul says this kind of fear does not come from God. Rather, it looks into circumstances or the future and imagines God not being there. We are told not to give in to it.

On the positive side, Paul says that God does give us a spirit of "power and love." Think through the decisions facing you. Wouldn't you feel much more confident about your actions if you could make decisions being absolutely convinced that your Father's love superintends your actions and that His power enables you to move forward with them? The reality is that you do have that spirit. It is His Spirit, which God has given you.

Face each day with the certainty that the Spirit living in you will guide your steps. Don't live with analysis paralysis. Act in faith that your life is being animated by Christ and that, because of that, you cannot fail.

Foot Washing

*He who has bathed needs only to wash
his feet, but is completely clean.*

JOHN 13:10

When Jesus tried to wash His disciple Peter's feet, Peter said no. Jesus responded that he was not going to experience authentic life with Jesus unless he allowed it. "Then wash me all over!" was Peter's answer. Today's verse was Jesus' response to Peter.

The point He was making was that Peter wasn't a dirty person. He simply had dirt on him at that moment that needed to be wiped off. There is a big difference between the two. Do you see it? Just because you sometimes get dirt (sinful thoughts, feelings, or even actions) on you doesn't mean that you've morphed into a dirty person.

I encourage you not to think of yourself as a dirty person who can't be used by God. Everyone blows it at times, but that doesn't change the fact that, at the core of your being, you are clean because of what Christ has done for you. Maybe you need your feet to be washed off right now. But that doesn't make you a dirty person.

Don't cheat yourself out of the thrill of living in the carefree abandon of faith by walking in dirt. Don't entertain deceptive feelings that you're unworthy to be made clean by Jesus. You are worthy because He has chosen you.

Numbered Days

Teach us to number our days,
That we may present to You a heart of wisdom.

PSALM 90:12

Once a day is past, it can never be reclaimed. How you spend the time you have in this world is an important matter. Our days are a commodity that can be spent to bring honor to God and great blessing to the lives of others and us.

We mark the days on a calendar, looking forward to an event. But we are also marking off the days behind. We can never recapture them. How do you want to spend each day? If days were money to be spent, how carefully would you contemplate spending each one?

God's plan for you is to lead you forward so you don't leave this world with a multitude of regrets. You have the potential to live the kind of life that will stand as an ongoing tribute to the goodness and grace of God.

We become wise in our approach to life as we realize we won't be here forever. Don't allow others to control your time. Decide for yourself how to be a wise steward of the days you have left in this world. Investing them well will leave a legacy that honors Him and blesses others.

Wiped-Out Sins

I have wiped out your transgressions like a thick cloud,
And your sins like a heavy mist.
Return to Me, for I have redeemed you.

Isaiah 44:22

Imagine for a moment that you had never done anything to feel guilty about. Wouldn't that be fantastic? What if any and every wrong thing you'd ever done had never happened? Would that empower you to live more boldly, with more confidence that God's plan is to bless you in all you do? Would it be a motivation to enjoy intimacy with your Father at every moment?

Grace brings news to you that seems almost too good to be true. It's this—your sins have been wiped out as if they had never happened. They are gone and forgotten by God. When God looks at you, He sees you as if you never sinned. Does that seem too good to be true? "How could that be?" you might ask.

The answer is that it is possible because of what Jesus did when He came the first time. He dealt a blow to sin that didn't simply defeat it; the deathblow against sin through the cross annihilated it in your life. There is not even a trace of it left now. "Return to me," God says, "because I have already wiped out your sins."

Horrible Choices

Where can I go from Your Spirit?
Or where can I flee from Your presence?
If I ascend to heaven, You are there;
If I make my bed in Sheol, behold, You are there.

PSALM 139:7-8

Your God will never abandon you. David said, "If I make my bed in Sheol [Hebrew for "the grave," but rendered in some translations as "hell"], behold, You are there." Somebody may say, "But I've created my own living hell. I may as well be a dead man. How can I possibly move forward from here?"

The answer is this: God is there with you in the hell you created. Trust Him! He will lead you out and guide you. Don't believe the lie that you have forfeited God's best for your life because of wrong choices you've made. Trust your Father instead.

You may argue, "My decision was intentionally wrong. I decided to do it. How could God work in this?" Before you were ever born, God saw everything from start to finish. He saw every decision you were ever going to make. Based on His sovereign decrees, every decision you were to make in your lifetime was incorporated into the master plan.

Your Father is a redeemer of bad situations. Yield yourself and your circumstances to Him. His grace still offers miracles.

Getting Well

When Jesus saw him lying there, and knew that
he had already been a long time in that condition,
He said to him, "Do you wish to get well?"

John 5:6

Before the paralyzed man by the Pool of Bethesda
was healed, he had to come face-to-face with a question that, on the surface, seems bizarre. "Do you want
to get well?" Jesus asked him. "Do I want to get well?"
the man might have exclaimed. "What kind of question is that? Of course I want to get well!"

That's not what he said. Instead he began to explain
why being well was outside the realm of possibility for
him. Somewhere along the way, his dream of ever walking again had died. Jesus, however, is in the business of
resurrecting things that have died. With loving compassion, He simply said to the man, "Get up." Inherent
in His word was both the motivation and the ability for
the man to finally do what his heart had yearned to do
for years—to walk.

What has died in you? What debilitates you in your
grace walk? You can be well. God's will is most definitely for you to know and believe this fact—it's your
turn! Jesus is speaking to you right now. Deep inside
you something is stirring. It is a hope that all this might
be true. Well, it is.

And Suddenly

And suddenly there came from heaven a noise
like a violent rushing wind, and it filled
the whole house where they were sitting.

ACTS 2:2

Don't ever lose hope about your Father moving in an area that concerns you. Things could change in your life in a moment. God has a way of acting suddenly. After the disciples had waited in the upper room for ten days, *suddenly* everything changed.

Don't worry about obstacles either. In an instant, they can be removed and life can turn around. Don't think that your life will always be like it is now. Believe God for His blessings. Never give up on Him. He indeed does love you and has a wonderful plan for your life.

Maybe you've lived life on the same track for many years. You've thought about your dreams, but they have seemed impossible. After all, considering your circumstances, how could things be different?

Don't judge your future by your past. If you sense that God's will for you requires a change, know that it can happen at any moment. Change will come. Live with faith-led expectancy. It might be today. If not today, it might be tomorrow. Keep persevering and trusting God because He is good and certainly will act on your behalf.

Clothed with Christ

*All of you who were baptized into Christ
have clothed yourselves with Christ.*

GALATIANS 3:27

Through the work of the cross, Jesus has become your suit of spiritual clothes. He has taken away your rags of religion and given you the garment of grace. You are "well suited" to be an ambassador for Christ in this world.

Many people are trying to dress themselves up with religious behavior, but their attempt is wasted. Jesus said to the church at Laodicea,

> Because you say, "I am rich, and have become wealthy, and have need of nothing," and you do not know that you are wretched and miserable and poor and blind and naked, I advise you to buy from Me gold refined by fire so that you may become rich, and white garments so that you may clothe yourself, and that the shame of your nakedness will not be revealed (Revelation 3:17-18).

Religion is man's attempt to look good to God. Grace is God's goodness clothing you through Christ. See Jesus when you look in the mirror.

Don't Sweat It

Linen turbans shall be on their heads and
linen undergarments shall be on their
loins; they shall not gird themselves with
anything which makes them sweat.

EZEKIEL 44:18

This particular verse in Ezekiel teaches a valuable lesson that still applies to our lives today. The priests were to wear linen because the fabric was light and didn't cause them to sweat.

The pattern there sets the course for every servant of God throughout history. Our Father's plan is that, metaphorically speaking, we should never sweat. Do we serve Him? Yes, of course, but we don't work out of our own ability. Our efforts are an expression of His life operating in and through us.

Legalism commends endless service, even to the point of exhaustion. In the grace walk, we aren't passive—but because we don't depend on ourselves as the energy source for service, we are able to serve endlessly and tirelessly.

If your spiritual service causes you to feel fatigued, perhaps your actions aren't coming from the proper source. As we serve God in the power of the Spirit, much is accomplished. But our strength is renewed, not depleted.

Harsh Criticism

The scribes who came down from Jerusalem were saying, "He is possessed by Beelzebul," and "He casts out the demons by the ruler of the demons."

MARK 3:22

Don't be surprised when hyper-religious people criticize you when you speak about the pure grace of God. When Jesus came into his public ministry professing to be teaching who God is, the religious leaders of His day were outraged. The God He described in no way fit the traditional viewpoint they had held. And this started with the familiarity with which Jesus talked about God—calling Him *Abba* to a group of people who dared not even speak His name at all.

Almost everything Jesus did dropped a grace-bomb on them. He wreaked havoc on their religious system. He did more than turn over the tables in the temple. That was mild compared to how He turned over the tables of tainted tradition they regarded as sacred doctrines. He is doing the same thing in the religious world today.

In confronting the leaders' faulty notions about who God is, Jesus often revealed the Father in a way that highlighted the stark contrast between their religious viewpoints and spiritual reality. Your grace walk probably won't have the approval of every religious person you know. Remember that you're in good company. They didn't approve of Jesus either.

Created for Relationship

*In the beginning God created the
heavens and the earth.*

GENESIS 1:1

The first verse of the Bible implies an important truth that will affect your grace walk as much as anything possibly could. The word *God* is plural in the original Hebrew text. In the very first verse of the Bible there is an immediate implied reference to the Father, Son, and Holy Spirit.

Why is this triune aspect of God important? Because it sets forth from the beginning that our God is first and foremost relational. The love that exists between the Father, Son, and Holy Spirit is the most important and foundational truth we can speak about God. John said, "God is love" (1 John 4:8). It is only when we understand the loving interaction between the Father, Son, and Spirit that we will find our grace walk headed in the right direction.

You have been created to live in relationship. The most important relationship you will experience is to be a child of God. Beyond that, your life is interconnected with others. Value the relationships you have in this world. Nurture them, knowing that they find their roots in God Himself.

Self-Consciousness

The eyes of both of them were opened, and they
knew that they were naked; and they sewed fig
leaves together and made themselves loin coverings.

GENESIS 3:7

Before Adam and Eve ate from the Tree of the Knowledge of Good and Evil, they were naked and not ashamed. They walked with God every day without inhibition. Their focus was on Him, and they found all meaning in the union they shared with Him.

When they ate from the forbidden tree, everything instantly changed. One of the most telling consequences of their disobedience is found in this verse: "They knew that they were naked and they sewed fig leaves together and made themselves loin coverings." Suddenly, people no longer felt comfortable or acceptable before God. Self-consciousness filled Adam and Eve's minds.

As you walk in grace, set your focus on your Lord and not on yourself. To allow yourself to be self-conscious will affect you just as it did Adam and Eve. It will cause you to feel inadequate and provoke an inner sense that you need to do something to be presentable to Him.

You are presentable and completely accepted by your Father. Don't let anything cause you to look away from Him so that you become bogged down in self-condemnation. He has seen you since He created you and loves you just as you are.

One Mediator

*There is one God, and one mediator also
between God and men, the man Christ Jesus.*

1 Timothy 2:5

Jesus became a man to unite Himself with mankind and act as the conduit through which we enter into Divine Life. He has situated us in the embrace of the Trinity. Today, there is a man in heaven among the Godhead who mediates our earthly lives.

In Christ Jesus, we will throughout eternity enjoy the experiences He has with His Father through the fellowship of the Spirit. That has been the plan from the beginning. The incarnation of Christ makes no sense apart from that plan. He is the One who has brought us back together with the Father.

As the God-man, Jesus knows what it is to be human. He has lived in your world and faced the same pressures and temptations that you face. He also knows what it is to be Deity. He has eternally lived in union with the Father and the Spirit.

He lives inside you now to mediate the life of God through your humanity. You are an expression of Him in your own unique form. You haven't been deified, but you do possess Him at the core of your nature.

Live each day as a person in whom divinity resides. Jesus' divine life will act through your humanity to reveal the Father's life and love to all you meet.

Fulfilled Promises

As many as are the promises of God, in Him
they are yes; therefore also through Him is
our Amen to the glory of God through us.

2 CORINTHIANS 1:20

You stand in a much better place today than Old Testament saints ever knew. They lived by the promises of God, but you don't. Today's verse shows that God made many promises and that they are all fulfilled in Jesus Christ. He is the final "yes!" to all that the Father has promised.

Speaking of the saints of old, the Bible says,

All these, having gained approval through their faith, did not receive what was promised, because God had provided something better for us, so that apart from us they would not be made perfect.

They didn't see all God's promises fulfilled in their lifetime, but your Father has "provided something better" for you.

You have Jesus in you. Every promise of God has been fulfilled in Him. Your only response is to say "Amen!"—which means "Yes!"—to those fulfilled promises. You aren't standing on the promises. You are seated on the premises of fulfilled promises in Christ.

Wilderness Roadways

Do not call to mind the former things, or
ponder things of the past. Behold, I will do
something new, now it will spring forth; will
you not be aware of it? I will even make a
roadway in the wilderness, rivers in the desert.

ISAIAH 43:18-19

We tend to imagine the future based on our past experiences. Then our past becomes the mental framework within which we envision what lies ahead.

If unwise choices in your past seem to have affected your potential for the future, you are particularly vulnerable to the risk of this false perspective. This outlook displaces faith because it limits your expectations of what God can and will do in the coming days.

Don't allow yourself to become bogged down in the past. Your best days are still ahead. Our God doesn't live in the past. He is the great "I Am" who lives in you at this moment and leads you forward to new vistas of divine opportunities.

Perhaps you have made decisions that seem to limit future possibilities. It is important to recognize that God transcends natural circumstances and isn't restricted by what you face. He has the power to "make a roadway in the wilderness" when it comes to obstacles in your situation. Your future is a new day in which your Loving Father already has planned your steps.

No Revival Necessary

Having such a hope, we use great boldness in our speech, and are not like Moses, who used to put a veil over his face so that the sons of Israel would not look intently at the end of what was fading away.

2 Corinthians 3:12-13

There is never a time when you need revival in your life. You are neither sick nor dead. You are alive in Christ, and His life never wanes.

Revival is an Old Testament concept. It isn't mentioned even once in the New Testament. Under the system of Law the people needed to be revived repeatedly because the glory of God faded among them. The Bible says the glory on the face of Moses "was fading away."

In this New Covenant of grace in which you live, there is no ebb and flow of divine power or presence. The only need we have today is to receive the revelation of what Paul called "Christ in you, the hope of glory." To realize that Jesus Christ lives inside you and that He will never leave you is all you need.

The indwelling Christ will sustain you at every moment and in every situation. Whenever you feel weak or even distant from God, remember that what you need isn't revival but a greater revelation of who He is in you and who you are in Him. The union you share with Christ never weakens or decreases.

The Message of Grace

I commend you to God and to the word of His grace,
which is able to build you up and to give you the
inheritance among all those who are sanctified.

ACTS 20:32

When leaving the city of Ephesus, the apostle Paul spoke one final word to the friends he loved and had led in that church. He told them that he commended them to God and to the message of His grace. The apostle Paul had spent three years teaching them the good news of grace and now, as he was leaving, he reassured them. It was through that message that God would build them up and cause them to experience the inheritance that was their spiritual birthright.

There are many trendy topics in the church world today, but never lose sight of the fact that it is the message of God's grace that will cause you to grow spiritually and to live the life He intends for you to experience. Grace isn't just another subject in the Bible. It is *the* subject—because grace is the fountainhead from which everything that can be known about our God springs.

Examine every biblical topic through the lens of the Father's grace expressed in Jesus Christ through the Spirit. Any other approach will leave you with nothing but dead doctrine. It is the message of Living Grace that will build you up and equip you in life.

A New Day

God called the light day, and the darkness
He called night. And there was evening
and there was morning, one day.

GENESIS 1:5

If you were asked to name the parts of a day, what would you say? Most people would list morning, afternoon, and night. But that's not the way the Bible identifies a day. When God created all things, the Scripture indicates that the evening came first in a new day.

Most people think new days begin when things start to get light. God doesn't order a full day that way. The Jewish faith recognizes that although the Sabbath is Saturday, it begins at sunset on Friday evening. That is the start of the new day—the Sabbath Day.

If things seem to be getting darker in your life, be encouraged that this may be the beginning of a new day in life. We all like to see the light begin to shine, but remember that your Father starts a new time when it begins to get dark.

Don't become discouraged if you have prayed for Him to work in your circumstances and it seems things are getting darker. That may point to the answer to your prayer. Just keep trusting Him, and in His time, the light will shine again.

Fear Not

*He said, "I heard the sound of You in
the garden, and I was afraid."*

GENESIS 3:10

One of the immediate results of sin's entering the world was that man became filled with fear. Fear is the painful emotion we experience when we anticipate that something dangerous is about to happen to us. It can debilitate us.

Jesus continuously told his disciples to "fear not." Throughout history, the plague of fear that began in the Garden of Eden has continually threatened the possibility of a fulfilled life for people. Only eternity will reveal the potential that was squelched by fear in people's lives.

You don't have to live with fear. You can rise above it for one reason: the One who has conquered fear is the One who lives in you and equips you for everything you will face in life. Almighty God is the origin of your life. He is the One who sustains, guides, and protects you.

Whatever may be threatening you in your life right now, "Fear not." He is with you. You will move through this lifetime with God on your side.

Grace, Grace!

This is the word of the LORD to Zerubbabel saying, "Not by might nor by power, but by My Spirit," says the LORD of hosts. "What are you, O great mountain? Before Zerubbabel you will become a plain; and he will bring forth the top stone with shouts of 'Grace, grace to it!'"

ZECHARIAH 4:6-7

When the angel of God spoke about the obstacles that Zerubbabel would face in rebuilding the temple, He reminded him that the progress made wouldn't be a result of his own might or power but because of the Spirit of God. Spiritual barriers are never overcome by sheer human willpower. Our source is His Spirit, not our own strength.

What is the means by which we level the mountains of opposition that threaten our reaching the goals our God has given us? It is grace—the divine enablement of His Spirit within us. As you survey the mountain that lies before you, compare its size to God, not your personal strength. Zerubbabel did and, with that perspective, could cry out, "What are you, O great mountain?"

God assured him that he would overcome it with shouts of "Grace, grace to it!" Speak grace into the towering obstacles of your life and watch what His power can accomplish. Grace is always your strength, whatever you face in life.

Dead to Sin

What shall we say then? Are we to continue in sin
so that grace may increase? May it never be! How
shall we who died to sin still live in it? Or do you
not know that all of us who have been baptized into
Christ Jesus have been baptized into His death?

ROMANS 6:1-3

A great misunderstanding about the grace walk is this: believers who focus so strongly on the grace of God make little of sinful actions. The accusations often suggest that we are making it easy for people to sin by stressing grace so strongly. The concern is that people may go too far with grace and do sinful things, using the excuse that grace will cover it.

Paul was accused of teaching such a message. He responded to the charge by pointedly asking in this text, "How shall we who died to sin still live in it?" The point he was making is that it simply isn't possible.

You died with Jesus on the cross, being "baptized into His death." You don't have a sin nature. The Adamic nature died with Jesus. When you were raised with Him, you were raised with His nature—the nature of righteousness.

Don't worry about grace leading to sinful behavior. Don't listen to those who make such foolish accusations either. You have been immersed into His death and now continually live in His life. That won't lead to sin. Never!

Love Controls Us

The love of Christ controls us…
2 Corinthians 5:14

The apostle Paul made a statement here that stands in contradiction to a popular message of legalistic religion. It is often taught today that our love for Christ should control us and cause us to behave. We're told the problem is that we don't love Jesus enough and that we simply need to love Him more.

In this verse, Paul spoke in opposite terms. He suggested that it isn't our love for Christ that regulates our actions, but His love for us. He didn't say it was his love *for* Christ but the love *of* Christ that controlled him.

Don't constantly grade yourself on how much you love Him. Instead, focus on how much He loves you. To shift your focus in that way will bring miraculous change. As you grow in understanding how much He loves you, that knowledge will transform your desires and motivation so you find yourself *wanting* to live in a way that honors Him. Put your focus in the right place—off yourself and on Jesus—and watch what happens.

Diversity in the Body

*There are varieties of ministries, and the same
Lord...For even as the body is one and yet has many
members, and all the members of the body, though
they are many, are one body, so also is Christ.*

1 Corinthians 12:5,12

Our Father loves diversity. But dead, legalistic religion insists on uniformity. The apostle Paul stressed that although there is great diversity within the body of Christ, we all share the same Head. Jesus Christ gives life to each part of His body, as diverse as the members may be.

Beware of making quick judgments about those whose walk with Christ doesn't look exactly like yours. There are liturgical members of the body, mainline evangelical members of the body, charismatic members of the body, and other members who might be described with other terms.

The issue isn't what the members of Christ's body look like. The central matter rests in the fact that we draw our life from Jesus Christ, the Head. We can learn from each other through our differences. We can bless each other with our differences.

Different doesn't mean someone is wrong. It just means they are different. Accept the whole body, and let's glorify the Head together.

Approved Works

Go then, eat your bread in happiness and drink your
wine with a cheerful heart;
for God has already approved your works.

ECCLESIASTES 9:7

Religious bondage keeps people in the place where they are continually examining their religious service to be sure the work is consistent enough, sacrificial enough, big enough, strong enough, effective enough, and so on. The list goes on and on and on. The gnawing question is always, "Is it enough?"

The grace walk is a lifestyle in which people can relax and enjoy living. They don't have to be concerned about whether their works are enough to please God, because they understand that their Father is pleased *with them.* They know that works are simply the outflow of the intimate and loving relationship they share together with God.

Which lifestyle are you living right now? Here's great news: you have divine permission to relax, enjoy your relationship to God, and let your good works flow naturally out of you. Because the Spirit of Christ is at work in you, He will also be at work *through* you to accomplish the Father's purposes.

Your works are actually His works through you, so you don't have to examine them. Just enjoy them and thank Him for working through you.

Earthen Vessels

We have this treasure in earthen vessels, so
that the surpassing greatness of the power
will be of God and not from ourselves.

2 Corinthians 4:7

You possess a tremendous treasure—an amazing reality that causes angels to stare at you in bewilderment. It is a treasure given to you in Christ.

What is this treasure? It is the power of God that lives inside you through the person of Jesus Christ. The Word who spoke the universe into existence dwells in you, a human being! Mighty Deity and meager humanity have become one because Jesus has joined us in union with His Father.

Why would God place such infinite power within our frail human bodies? So that when He works through us, it will be obvious that this miraculous life we live doesn't originate from us, but from Him. The greatness of Almighty God is seen as He lives through one of His fragile but dearly loved people.

Don't expect anything from yourself. You're just a container made of mud. However, expect much from God because He takes great pleasure in the fact that His life and yours are one. He delights in expressing Himself through you.

Feeling Love

Looking at him, Jesus felt a love for him…
MARK 10:21

The tenth chapter of Mark records the story of the rich young ruler. He came to Jesus asking how to inherit eternal life. Knowing that his love of money was the god of his life, Jesus told him to sell everything he had and give the money to the poor. The Bible says the man went away grieving, unwilling to part with his fortune.

Mark makes a telling observation about the situation. He wrote, "Looking at him, Jesus felt a love for him." Jesus knew what the young man's reaction would be. He watched the man walk away and reject Him. Yet He felt love for him. This statement shows the heart of God as much as anything could. Even knowing that the man loved his money more than anything, Jesus still felt a love for him.

Religious judgmentalism would have us believe that God feels offended and maybe even angry when people love something else more than they love Him. Jesus showed us differently. Our God looks on hurting humanity and pities those who are blind. Sins won't sicken Him. They sadden Him. When people reject Him, He doesn't leave them. He loves them.

Look carefully at the attitude and actions of Jesus in this story. Then see others through His eyes. Show no condemnation toward others, but only compassion.

Hopeless Moments

When He heard that he was sick, He then stayed
two days longer in the place where He was.

JOHN 11:6

When the sisters of Lazarus sent word to Jesus that their brother was deathly ill, Jesus stayed where He was for two more days. When He finally arrived in Bethany, Lazarus was already dead. The sisters were distraught. Martha even lashed out at him: "If You had been here, my brother would not have died. Even now I know that whatever You ask of God, God will give You."

Martha's emotions are those we all feel at times. We see ourselves in an urgent situation that desperately needs divine intervention. We ask Jesus to help, but it seems He is nowhere to be found. Then the situation deteriorates until it seems beyond help.

In those moments, it isn't uncommon to think like Martha: "Lord, you could have helped if you *would* have helped!" Jesus can handle our negative emotional reactions. But don't stop there. Martha went on to say, "Even now I know that whatever you ask of God, God will give you."

On the heels of her broken feelings was her bold faith. When you face a situation that seems hopeless, don't lose hope. Your God hasn't forgotten you. Even now He can work in your situation. Look to Him and trust for His intended outcome.

The Message of Reconciliation

God was in Christ reconciling the world to Himself,
not counting their trespasses against them, and He
has committed to us the word of reconciliation.

2 Corinthians 5:19

The good news of the gospel is summarized in this single verse. Through the finished work of the cross, you have been reconciled to God, and your trespasses will never be effective against you again. In the power of the Spirit, our God has united us to Himself in Jesus. Nothing can change what was accomplished on the cross.

It isn't your faith or commitment, nor is it your consistency or conduct, that establishes this position of union with God. It is true because the work of the cross was not a failure. Sin was defeated, and you were rescued and restored to God there.

When we know that our sin can never again intimidate us because it truly is gone, we are then free to take the message of reconciliation and share the good news with others. There is no greater joy than to see somebody else trust Christ and receive what He has already done for them.

Rejoice in your own position in Christ. Then ask the Holy Spirit to guide you to others who are hungry to know this good news. Many are waiting for you to tell them what Jesus has done for them and the great benefit He has brought to us all.

Resisting Legalism

It was because of the false brethren secretly brought in, who had sneaked in to spy out our liberty which we have in Christ Jesus, in order to bring us into bondage. But we did not yield in subjection to them for even an hour, so that the truth of the gospel would remain with you.

GALATIANS 2:4-5

When you walk in the liberty of Christ Jesus, you will encounter people along the way who will disapprove. They will think that you are too relaxed about your walk; that you don't take devotion to God seriously enough; that you need to become more like them. Beware of these people.

The gospel is the good news that Jesus Christ has done all that needs to be done to put you in good standing with your Father. He couldn't be more proud of you. While the legalistic messages that urge sacrifice, commitment, self-denial, and personal discipline may sound appealing on the surface, there is always one way you can know they're a lie that leads to bondage. They point to you—to your efforts.

Grace encompasses sacrifice, commitment, self-denial, and personal discipline—and lays them in the lap of Jesus, allowing the gospel of grace to govern life. Don't yield to the subtle lies of legalistic teaching—not even for an hour.

The Price of Unbelief

*We see that they were not able to
enter because of unbelief.*

Hebrews 3:19

The reason it took Israel 40 years to enter Canaan wasn't because of the distance from Egypt. They should have been able to make that trip in a few weeks. Instead they wandered in the wilderness for four decades, unable to enter the Promised Land.

God had already given them the land. He wasn't waiting to give it to them when they arrived—it had been theirs since the day He had said so. However, their experience didn't align with God's reality. And we're told they couldn't enter in because of unbelief.

The same thing happens today. The Father has given us everything we need in Jesus Christ. Forgiveness, reconciliation, and justification—the list could go on in naming the benefits provided through the finished work of Christ on the cross. The question is not what you have. The question revolves around what you have accepted by faith.

Don't miss the land of abundant living that has been given to you in Christ. Believe Him now and possess the land! It's all yours in Him. Put away all doubt and denial and simply enjoy new life in Him.

A New Covenant

*If that first covenant had been faultless, there
would have been no occasion sought for a second...
When He said, "A new covenant," He has made
the first obsolete. But whatever is becoming
obsolete and growing old is ready to disappear.*

Hebrews 8:7,13

God's Law is perfect, but the Old Covenant of Law
wasn't perfect. The Bible says that if it had been faultless there would have been no need for the New Covenant. The Law was perfect for revealing man's sin, but it
had absolutely no power to remedy the problem. It was
a diagnostician with no cure for a fatal disease.

The New Covenant of grace in Jesus Christ has
replaced the old system of laws. The old has become
obsolete. It is yesterday's news; it has been worn out and
set aside. (That's what the word *obsolete* means.)

Religious voices of our day still direct people toward
the Law as a means of honoring God, but their message contradicts what the Bible teaches. You have Jesus
living inside you, showing you new ways of living and
generating within you a desire to live His life in this
world.

The "old school" way of doing things is done. That
school has been eternally closed. It's summer vacation
in Christ, and this vacation will never end.

The Fear of Judgment

She said to Elijah, "What do I have to do with you,
O man of God? You have come to me to bring my
iniquity to remembrance and to put my son to death!"

1 Kings 17:18

When Elijah showed up at the house of a widow whose son was terribly sick, she became afraid when she saw the prophet. She imagined he had come to her because of her sins and that her son would now die as punishment. That's how the Old Covenant mentality always works.

Perhaps you have been in legalistic environments that have left you with a mental attitude that anticipates judgment by God. You can relax. That day doesn't exist for you. You are in Christ, and there is no condemnation to you.

Elijah actually acted as a type of Jesus in this instance. The woman's son didn't die. Instead, he was healed through the prophet's ministry. Throughout the Old Testament Scriptures there are glimpses of grace like this.

Jesus didn't come to visit retribution upon you. He came to rescue you and restore you to humanity's original innocence before the Father. He accomplished that so that you never need to fear Him.

Your True Self

*The angel of the LORD appeared to him and said to
him, "The LORD is with you, O valiant warrior."
Then Gideon said to him, "O my lord, if the LORD
is with us, why then has all this happened to us?
And where are all His miracles which our fathers
told us about, saying, 'Did not the LORD bring us
up from Egypt?' But now the LORD has abandoned
us and given us into the hand of Midian."*

JUDGES 6:12-13

Gideon was a small man in the smallest tribe of
Israel. When God called him to lead the people in battle, his own sense of inadequacy flooded his thoughts
and feelings. Note how the Angel of the Lord addressed
him: "The LORD is with you, O valiant warrior."

God sees things about you that you may not see
or know about yourself. He saw Gideon's true identity when the man himself didn't see it at all. He knows
the same about you. Believe what He says about you
in Scripture. Embrace and act on the identity He has
given you, regardless of whether you feel it or think it.
What God says about you is true. You can base your
actions on your true identity even when your emotions
contradict the truth.

Good Plans

*"I know the plans that I have for you," declares
the Lord, "plans for welfare and not for
calamity to give you a future and a hope."*

Jeremiah 29:11

The people of Israel were enduring captivity in Babylon when the Lord spoke these words to them through the prophet Jeremiah. After they had lived in harsh adversity, the promise was probably hard for some of them to believe. Bitter experiences have the potential to jade people's perspective and cause them to become cynical about the future.

Whatever you may have experienced in your own life, don't make the mistake of projecting negative faith into your future. The brightest and best days lie ahead for you. The first song I learned in life was called "Every Day with Jesus Is Sweeter Than the Day Before." It's true. While outward circumstances may vary, your walk with Christ will only become better and better, culminating at the time when you finally see Him face-to-face.

Don't anticipate negative days in this temporal world either. Presume upon the goodness of God. He is honored when you have faith in His lovingkindness. He has plans for you, and they are good. Believe it and anticipate it.

Everlasting Love

The LORD appeared to him from afar, saying,
"I have loved you with an everlasting love;
Therefore I have drawn you with lovingkindness."

JEREMIAH 31:3

Before anything material took shape or form, the love of God toward you was an eternal reality. The beauty of all the beaches, mountains, and forests of the world pales in comparison to the beauty of His everlasting love. All the stars and planets in their grandeur bow in the presence of the eternal love of God—the love that was set on you before there was a flicker of light in the universe.

His love for you has no beginning. His love has always existed within the shared love of the Trinity. Father, Son, and Spirit reveled in their plan to bring you into existence and into the circle of divine union they had forever known. You are not an afterthought in creation.

You have been drawn to God by divine intention and through divine passion. Never, never, never entertain the thought that He doesn't care. The love He has for you will endure throughout eternity. Set aside shame about the past, guilt about the present, and worry about the future. Divine Love holds you tenderly in His arms and will never let you go, even for a moment.

A Word from the Author

If reading *Grace Walk Moments* has helped you, I would be happy to hear from you. It is always encouraging for an author to receive feedback from those who have read his books. You may write me at the following address:

Dr. Steve McVey
Grace Walk Ministries
PO Box 6537
Douglasville, GA 30135

You may also e-mail me at info@gracewalk.org. I invite you to visit our ministry website at www.grace walk.org, where you can learn more about our ministry around the world. Every week, on our home page I post the "Sunday Preaching Program," a 30-minute teaching from the Bible that guides you in how to live each day in the loving grace of your Father. The teachings are free and are always practical to daily living.

You can also connect with me through my blog, at www.stevemcvey.com, as well as through Facebook. My goal on these sites is to share details from both my ministry and day-to-day life in order to connect with readers more personally.

I have written numerous other books besides this one, including the bestselling *Grace Walk*. Those books, as well as a wide variety and CDs and DVD teachings I have produced, are available through the online store accessible through gracewalk.org. I invite you to visit our store to browse the many other writings and records there that can help you in your own daily grace walk.

Finally, if *Grace Walk Moments* has encouraged you, would you share it with others? Many of us who believe that this message of grace needs to spread are teaming together to make it known to others.

How can you help? If you purchase a copy of this book through my office as a gift for somebody else, I will be happy to autograph the copy you purchase. Another way to help bring visibility to the book is to post positive reviews on online sites that sell the book, such as amazon.com and other retailers.

Together we can reach out to encourage people with the transforming power of the gospel of grace. It isn't self-effort or magic formulas that transform people. It is the living presence of Jesus Christ. Join me in making this message known, and then stay in contact with me to let me know what our Father is doing through you to reach others with the wonderful news of His transforming love!

Also by Steve McVey

The Grace Walk Devotional

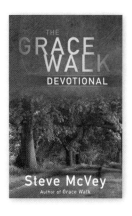

There's no better way to start your day than to let God remind you of His love and all-encompassing generosity and grace.

These devotions from Steve McVey will point you to Scripture and remind you to leave behind performance- and fear-based Christianity. They'll help you grasp anew that God's grace is immensely more than a doctrine—it's how He operates the universe. And He's invited you to enjoy it with Him!

Walking in the Will of God
Discovering the Grace and Freedom of His Plan for You

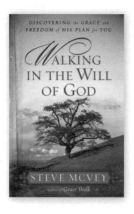

Wouldn't it be great to find out that God doesn't want you stressed and anxious about your life? That He has made knowing His will simple?

You can relax—it's true. The God of the Bible isn't distant and manipulative. He's not a formula to figure out. Instead, He's a Father you can trust. And your grace-filled, relational Father *wants* to guide you. You're His child, and He wants to see you succeed.

Walking in the Will of God will help you understand who God is and how you can rest in the truth that He is on your side. The result? You'll be able to live a bold, no-regrets life—the kind of life every Christian wants. *Includes questions for thought and discussion.*